That Difficult Peace

That Difficult Peace

by Joost A M. Meerloo, M.D.

PUBLISHED BY CHANNEL PRESS, INC., GREAT NECK, NEW YORK

THAT DIFFICULT PEACE

Library of Congress Catalog Card Number: 61-17217

PRINTED IN THE UNITED STATES OF AMERICA

Contents

ONE *The Political Breathing Spell and the Cold War, 9*

TWO *The Fate of Man's Aggression, 15*

HOSTILITY HAS MANY FACETS
SUBLIMATION OF AGGRESSION
REPRESSION OF AGGRESSION
SCAPEGOATISM AND PROJECTION
WEREWOLVES AND COLORED SHIRTS
THE NAZI BEAST WAS THE HUMAN BEAST
THE STRATEGY OF CRIMINALIZATION
THE STRATEGY OF NON-AGGRESSION
AGGRESSION, HATE AND FEAR
AGGRESSION AND WAR

THREE *Prejudice, Our Daily Test, 45*

HOW TO APPROACH THE PROBLEM?
PREJUDICE AS AN EMOTIONAL BAROMETER OF THE COLLECTIVE PSYCHE
THE MEANING OF SELF-HATRED AND MASOCHISM
RACIALISM AND DISCRIMINATION AS PRETEXT
THE ETERNAL SCAPEGOAT
THE ROOTS OF INDIVIDUAL HATRED AND HOSTILITY

THE ETERNAL MISANTHROPE
COLLECTIVE HATRED
COLLECTIVE HATRED AND THE CONFUSING PRESSURE BY A MINORITY
LOW-BROW HATES HIGH-BROW
THE ROLE OF THE GROUP-PSYCHE AND GROUP COHESION
THE VARIATION IN GROUP COHESION
DISCRIMINATION AS A TOOL OF AGGRESSION
FEAR AND DISCRIMINATION
THE CONTAGIOUS ASPECTS OF DISCRIMINATION
THE FEARLESS DON'T HATE

FOUR *The New Technical Age, 95*

FIVE *What Ails Our Civilization?, 107*

OVERPOPULATION AND INCREASING INTER-HUMAN RIVALRY
THE CONTRAST
THE SHADOW OF THE MUSHROOM
THE PARADOX OF PEACE AND AGGRESSION
WE HATE AND WE LIKE DESTRUCTION
PACIFISM AND THE SEARCH FOR A COMMON MORAL BASE

SIX *Psychological Peacefare—The Forgotten Science, 145*

THE BATTLE ON TWO FRONTS
TRAINING FOR DEMOCRATIC FREEDOM
THE PARADOX OF FREEDOM AND LIBERTY
PSYCHOLOGY AS A GUIDE FOR DEMOCRACY
MAN'S DISTORTED COMPULSION TO FIGHT
WHAT IS PSYCHOLOGICAL WARFARE?
WARFARE WITH WORDS
ARE PEOPLE INFECTED WITH A SUGGESTION OF UNAVOIDABLE WAR?
WHAT CAN MODERN PSYCHOLOGY CONTRIBUTE?
TOWARD PSYCHOLOGICAL PEACEFARE

SEVEN *That Difficult Peace of Mind, 179*

NOTES, *189*

That Difficult Peace

CHAPTER ONE

The Political Breathing Spell and the Cold War

Since the end of World War II—in almost any given period of weeks or months—we have witnessed an almost continuous counterpoint of shock and promise in international affairs.

An emotional shock was felt all across the world, for example, after the abrupt disintegration of the Paris Summit Conference and the strange political theater at the United Nations in the fall of 1960. The psychological question arises: Was this widely-publicized diplomatic debacle and the multitude of other disasters that preceded and followed it merely representative of the hostile explosion of bad-humored politicians? Or was it the result of a well-planned, purposeful strategy on the part of the U.S.S.R.? An analysis of Soviet methods of psychological warfare as revealed in their "Document of Terror"[1] suggests the latter explanation. Russian international strategists, in following

[1] All references and notes appear on pages 189 and 190.

Pavlovian theory, intend to make use of both the disturbing-negative and the confusing-positive emotions in the wake of emotional shocks in order to promote greater vulnerability in the minds of their adversaries.

To strategists of the Pavlovian school, it matters little whether enemy reaction to a particular international incident is greater confidence, indignity, or increased fear. More important to them are the enemy's reactions during the period of respite, the "breathing spell" separating one political incident from another. The preliminary campaign of shock and intimidation serves to soften the mental backbone of the unaware adversary, and is called "enlightened terror." By keeping the mass-emotions of an adversary nation in repeated turmoil through so-called "fractionalized shocking," the enemy peoples can gradually be made more receptive to ideological submission.

The *peredishka,* the breathing spell that separates the waves of terror and repeated emotional shocks (the strategist might also call it euphemistically "the period of peaceful coexistence"), represents an advantageous time for implanting desired ideas and ideological patterns, since the anticipation of new forms of terror may lead to unconscious surrender as people relax and lower their critical barriers Indeed, it is known clinically that after emotional shock people are more submissive to suggestion and more vulnerable to persuasion by the enemy. During the breathing spell, the systematic hammering in of doctrines can have greatest effect.

It is important to be keenly aware of this concept of psychological warfare as a kind of cat-and-mouse play, and to realize that man's mind *can* be softened and manipulated. The various methods of personal or collective persuasion and relentless mental conditioning may not always succeed. But the clinical fact is that, unobtrusively, man's mind *can* be made to lower its critical barriers, and consequently to endorse ideas with which it originally did not agree. Even the political accusation is merely used to push the other into the role of denial, as if he were standing before the court of international public opinion, already *feeling* guilty only because he is accused and blamed.

Our contemporary system of communication is indeed such a complicated web of human interrelationships that we may call this epoch of press, radio and television, the Age of the Electronic, Verbal Manipulation of the Mind. The overflow of words and ideas threatens to drown us, and we must seek new, selective psychic barriers and defenses to keep our individual integrity intact.

Continuous physical and psychological conditioning of the mind is no illusion anymore New drugs prolong our life span; others help to lure us into passive equanimity. The surreptitious mental manipulation exerted by advertising and propaganda is continually reforming our system of values Beyond this are the more extreme methods of real brainwashing, genocide and menticide. A true science of mental manipulation definitely does exist, and to the practitioners of this science, man is viewed as merely a malleable robot.

The fact that our complex society requires an abundance of new social institutions also places a coercive imprint on those administrative manipulations. We all have to adjust ourselves frequently to the imprisoning cobweb of red tape and governmental officiousness. True, man has always been molded by his own epoch. Every society conditions its members into conforming beliefs and attitudes. At this time in history, however, the tools of persuasion and coercion have become more effective and all-encompassing than ever before.

The more that modifying forces exist *without* our being aware of them, the more does it become necessary to alert people against the possibility of passive surrender to the onslaught of dinned-in ideas.

Where can we find our freedom? Only in rebellion and nonconformism? Only in creative endeavor? Or will we feel free only by cynically construing and constructing our feelings of despair into a philosophy of existence? An inadvertent censorship exists even in a free democratic world, because of the limitation of man's means of communication and the consequent exhortation of the professional writer. In order to be heard and read, one has to take option for a certain group and to show acceptable skill in verbal expression.

Let us be specific; let us consider first the extremes of brainwashing and menticide. It is well known that prisoners in dictatorial hands have been induced to make false confessions and to betray their friends. We are apt to overlook, however, the fact that a comparable form of mental coercion, only a little slower in effect, can contaminate and influence groups, and nations, and eventually the whole world, by means of the rather simple persuasive methods of cold war and psychological warfare—*provided these methods of slow coercion are not well understood by their victims.* Those who have the means of communication in their hands, combined with the power to terrorize people, can gradually bring about mental submission. Political confusion and anxiety-producing emotionalism are part of the totalitarian strategy to make an adversary gradually more submissive.

Such is the actual ideological dilemma of our epoch The outlook is either a democratic freedom (this strange harmony of opposites)—or a mechanized slavery that in its ultimate aim may even go beyond the horror of nuclear annihilation. Only recognition, and a thorough and widespread understanding of the continual mental coercion to which we all can be subjected, will give us the opportunity to remain free-thinking, stubborn individuals.

Many victims of brainwashing and menticide could have been stronger, and could have been saved from the tragic battle with their own conscience, had they had a greater understanding of the strategy of the coercive enemy who wanted to control their thoughts. They could have faced the pressures with the strength of well-trained foreknowledge, one of the best mental defenses of the free individual.

In Paris and New York, Russian diplomats taught us a lesson in Pavlovian political strategy. They have done it since, in the Congo and in Cuba and in Berlin and in Laos. They will continue to do so. And then, during the subsequent breathing spells, they wait for their adversaries' softening-up in order to launch a new wave of emotionalism at a time when their persuasion will not be detected, and their slow coercion not be discovered.

Our age asks for a psychological stubbornness to save our souls from the onslaught of psychological and political warfare. We have to be firmly aware that no real breathing spell exists. We have to face ourselves and our alternatives.

CHAPTER TWO

The Fate of Man's Aggression

It is man's tragedy—and, at the same time, his heroic challenge—that he must fight his battles on two very different fronts

Of course, there are many dangers coming from the outside world: nature threatens man; the social system tries to overwhelm him; tyranny has to be fought. But often more overpowering are the dangers arising from man's inner world: man's instinctual drives, his destructiveness, his aggression, his will for power, his desire to be a tyrant himself.

It is a tragic delusion to speak of a final world war between capitalists and communists. Man is both a capitalist and a communist. Man is a tyrant and man is a slave. Man is drunk with power and man is submissive. All these various qualities live in one and the same man, and all these inner contradictions belong to the normal pattern of human behavior.

Psychologists must bring man's ambivalent patterns more into focus, so that, once and for all, people can see man clearly for what he is; so that, in understanding and accepting the contradictions of his character, man will be better able to mold them into a harmonious and controllable unity. People must learn to canalize the forces of evolution, and to be aware of the continually developing counterforces.

Preparedness for peace is a spiritual challenge. People can hide their heads in the sand; they can live behind useless Maginot lines with fortresses and fleets that protect them only from facing the real problems of the world—emanating from the inner problems of man.

This is the challenge of our time.

Every war is a dramatization of man's inner war, the externalization of his inner conflicts. Man feels temporarily relieved of tensions when there is outside trouble in the world. He can postpone finding a solution to his own conflicts as long as the outside world offers a more stirring emotional drama in which he can play a role.

Yet, it is a very expensive production that man stages in order periodically to relax his tensions. It is as if the world needed the great excitement and insanity of war in order to relieve itself temporarily of personal madness.

Statistical figures show that during war the number of neuropsychoses decreases. Man pays for this later with new fears and feelings of insecurity; after the war his neuroses break out in greater frequency. He only postpones his neurosis in order to experience more immediately the drama of war.

Modern psychology teaches us that other ways besides war exist of relieving man's inner tensions and aggressions But the first step is to face these problems, to recognize them for what they are, and to be aware of man's urge for self-destruction revealing itself in the ritualized convulsions of war.

—1—

My mind returns to Holland at the turn of the century. Our usual family outing was a walk through the woods to the beach, along a tree-lined road built in the seventeenth century by the Dutch poet and statesman, Constantyn Huyghens. Often when we were too tired to walk we traveled on a horse-drawn bus that brought us directly to the fishers' harbor.

At the woods' entrance were old palaces standing like dream-houses behind thick foliage. One day—it must have been around 1910—this fairy-tale landscape changed The trees and houses were torn down to make way for a huge building that was to be erected.

This break into my childhood dreams was the International Palace of Peace, a vast structure presented by Andrew Carnegie to the world as a symbol that war by weapons could be converted into war by conference. In 1913 the building was festively opened and given to the various governments of the world. Then came the initial onslaught of World War I.

My childhood fantasies had no room for such concepts as conferences or warfare by words. The word "peace" had somehow settled somewhere in my infantile mind as a desirable situation; but it had something to do with peace at home, with quiet in the family and days without tension.

I often went to look at the work on the new structure. And I was most impressed by the corner tower, looking out over the road leading into the woods. In my fantasy I had already solved the problem of international peace. If countries wanted to fight each other, they had to send their armies along this very road to the beach where I used to walk. In such an ominous situation, our Queen would mount cannons and machine guns high on the tower of peace, and would shoot down everybody who wanted to go to war. In my fantasy I had made a high fortress out of the Palace of Peace.

Such was my first cosmogony of war and peace, a sensible solution for an infantile mind.

Many years later I was to work in the library of the Palace of Peace, gathering my notes on the psychology of war and peace. This was at the time of the Nazi occupation of my country, during a bitterly cold winter. The warmth of the library was heightened by the zest of working at a book that might be helpful, even influential.

In the same library room several Nazi officers were working and gathering their own notes. Evidently the enemy and occupier needed his literary justifications just as much as we needed ours.

Once an animated discussion took place. It was near Christmas of 1940. At one moment we all needed to refer to the same old book written on the subject of international peace, a volume written ages ago by another Dutchman, Hugo Grotius. This led us to discuss the common subject.

Suddenly we were no longer enemies. In the common search for eternal values we had temporarily halted our mutual prejudices and stereotypes.

Yet I became truly aware, for the first time, of the bestial aggression in man during those days of the Nazi occupation of Holland. Until then I had been familiar with such aggression only theoretically—from books on history and psychopathology. And although psychoanalysis had made me wiser about man's repressed animal drives, man's pathological fury had remained for me a remote theoretical concept, something outside the realm of civilized man

Day after day in the streets, the Nazis and their political friends demonstrated open, unprovoked aggression—against their scapegoats, against women and children, against even inanimate objects. They were perpetually drunk with their weird fanaticism, and preoccupied with aggression and destruction. They had already begun unprovoked street-terror in their own country merely to imprint awe and fear on the German people.

Writing this, I remember: this is what can happen in man!

Many myths have been circulated about man's native pugnacity and predatory nature. Is man really a fighter or is he principally a lover of peace? Is the aggressive attitude imposed upon him by social habits, or are there continual innate explosions and incitements from within? I am afraid that this chapter will add further to the myth of man's untamable aggression, because the experience of war has colored my reflections.

Civilization shapes and distorts human drives and inhibits them as well. What we usually call aggressiveness in modern man is either connected with man's action for self-defense and his need for survival, or with a more primitive need for power, revenge and tremendous destruction. Man's provoked aggression in the service of self-assertion and self-defense is most understandable. We may say that it is man's general answer to such frustrations as lack of food, lack of love, lack of communication, lack of sexual satisfaction, lack of acceptance

Thus we are able to comprehend how, in the twentieth century—with its daily diet of fear, tension and dissatisfaction—man's restrained irritation and anger can accumulate until hate and the urge for retaliation and destruction break loose. For such internal accumulation of tension, people don't have to be consciously aware of the causes of their frustrations.

Many of us live in a culture of advertised deprivation. Business and industry, for example, stimulate desires in us that cannot be fulfilled for all the people. Many of these desires were completely unknown only a few decades ago. Advertisements have made the yearning for luxury items universal, brewing dissatisfaction and neurotic aggression further stimulated by the increasing urge for newer technological gadgets, greater material possessions and social prestige.

On the other hand, many young people find inadequate opportunities in this rapidly changing society for discharging their energy and initiative, and for securing the possessions and powers to which they believe themselves entitled. The older generation attempts to keep young people dependent and insecure much longer than in former years. Thanks to better hygiene, better medical treatment and better methods of production, the average expectancy of life is now over sixty years, while in 1800 it was about thirty-five years. The result is that the community is prejudiced in favor of authority and leadership by the middle-aged. Organized education has not only become a means of providing skill and wisdom, but also an unobtrusive means of psychic manipulation for keeping young people longer in bonds in order to mold them into conforming adepts. They are forced to work under the continued authority of their elders. The older generation often stands in the way of the hopes of the younger generation, thus interfering with their lives in an ambiguous, tension-provoking way. Many young men are left with no outlet for their energy and for their desire for mature responsibility. They cannot afford to get married at the time of their greatest mating urge, and are forced to remain dependent. And because of their own feelings of insecurity, too many parents want to live their children's lives.

A growing tension between the generations sometimes leads to wild, emotional explosions and juvenile delinquency. The younger people who suffer most (because they have no inkling of the changing world) become rebellious toward their elders, reacting to them with anger, aggression and vague non-conformism. Especially in families where there is no unit and no discipline, resentment and empty anger are aroused. Schism and fascism may result from such resentment.

The youngsters convert their feelings of failure into a cynical, "I don't care" attitude. The angry young men want to indulge in reckless adventure; they want to fight; they want expansion; they want excitement; they crave an outlet for their suppressed sexual drives. All their frustrated energy piles up in aggressive tension. In our world in transition, this pattern of youthful restlessness is international. Arrogance and gang-formation are the harassing signs of widespread frustration.

In addition to man's drive for acquisition, final establishment, prestige and power—which already make for an increased need for self-assertion and aggression—modern culture insists that every individual delay and sublimate his instinctual longings, to charge them up to a peak from which perhaps a more poignant delayed satisfaction can be derived. For example, social etiquette prescribes exacting rules for a civilized way of satisfying hunger. The culinary technique, the play at the dinner table, are directed at a delay of the oral drive mixed with intensified anticipation. It may also be interpreted as an instinctual defense against the feeling of disgust that results from a greedy oversatisfaction of man's own drive. Yet one of the greatest evils of our "ice cream" culture is *overeating*—usually to satisfy ununderstood deeper yearnings.

These examples are mentioned because distorted drives resulting from cultural repression are found even more in the sexual sphere. On the one hand we find men who are impotent before they even start to live independently. On the other extreme are those who explode and destroy at the first arousing of sex. The strategy of sex as an initiation to loving has still not been solved in our world of erotic taboos. Dating has become more an act of prestige than a cult of Eros.

Cultural delay, hesitation and overcharging of drives—any or all of which may ultimately lead to a higher form of lust and ecstasy—bring the human soul to peculiar fluctuations of feeling. If a drive is not satisfied, the tension accumulates and the instinctual hate toward such restriction grows until the tension may break through the walls of taboo and cultural restraint. At such a moment it is not the preservation of life that is sought, but only the release of tension, even to the point of self-destruction and suicide. Various roots of aggressiveness are related to these ambivalent feelings toward the instincts of life. There are two opposing fulfillments related to instinctual drives. One can either satisfy the urge immediately, or delay and cultivate and hypercharge the satisfaction in fantastic anticipation of romance and eternal happiness.

What happens, then, to the surplus aggression constantly stimulated in modern man? Part of it is sublimated into cultural outlets; part is resolved in the excitement of sports and festivals; part of it has no outlet and must be repressed. Most of the tension we find back in aggressive dreams and fantasies, or acted out more pleasantly in Western movies, or described in murder stories and sadistic comic books. Part of it may also be projected and discharged onto scapegoats—every gang war is a war against fictitious scapegoats—and part of it will be expressed in the much more vague mass-emotion of "mature" war-mongering and war. It is no wonder that war has a more popular appeal to frustrated people than peace

What we call in psychiatry man's neurotic aggression, his *destructiveness,* his sadistic and masochistic attitude toward the world of the living and non-living, is rather difficult to understand as a biological drive. It is a typical *human* attitude. Animals are not sadistic; they only charge when they are attacked or frustrated in gathering food. Man's rage may be explained as a reaction toward infantile feelings of dependence, stimulated by society over and over again; or it can be explained in Freud's terms, as a self-destructive force per se. It is a fight against objects persecuting man in a magic fantasy world, as we see in the cruel fairy tales of childhood. By destroying his fellow being, man increases his feelings of power in a magic way; he incorporates, as it were, the strength of the slain foe. However, social fear and rejection, both, build up more reasons for increased destructiveness and eventual self-destruction.

Important to the understanding of the strange, confusing quality of human aggression is Edmund Bergler's concept of *pseudo-aggression.*[1] This, he says, is a strategy of rage and aggression used not as a needed defense against dangers from outside, but only to prove to oneself that one is not meek and submissive. Although much of this self-deceptive process takes place in deep, unconscious layers of the psyche, many people have some inkling of this human show of pseudo-aggressiveness. As a matter of fact, this form of heroic showing off is part of a general process. Unconsciously, people want to be meek and dependent, submissive and obedient. Consciously, they want to assure themselves that they are not cowards; not meek; not the good, submissive boys. The resulting strategy and show of pseudo-aggression—the defense against inner inertia and masochism—gradually becomes a commitment. From now on, the meek must show themselves to be more tyrannical and more destructive. "You see," they proclaim inwardly, "I am not a coward after all!"

The riddle of man's neurotic aggression involves more than mere self-defense and the release of uncoordinated surplus energy. We often see it break out suddenly after periods of peaceful living and tense control of contrasting forces in the psyche. We may compare it with the release of energy from within the atom. In the human psyche, inner combustion—the rationale of which we don't know—is also possible. Perhaps it is related to the innate ambivalence and contrasting forces living in man. In pathological delusions, the act of destruction is often called for, in the belief that destruction of the foe increases some inner potentiality and capacity, as does the sex act.

Hostility has many facets

The act of being born is in itself experienced as a hostile exposure and, indeed, in many mammals, the young are rejected and left to die if they are too weak to reach the mother's nipples within a certain time. This rejection of the weak, however, is a meaningful self-defense of the flock lest the weak prevent the herd from making its "trek," and thus expose it to enemy animals which prey upon the weak.

With this biological example we are in the midst of the paradox about hostility and defense, for often hate and hostility act as tension-reducing devices. That is why I want to call attention to the human paradox that both hostility and love can be a mask and a defense.

I have in mind a man with whom I struggled for years in order to understand his hostility better. To his boss and his ex-wife, he represented the most hostile man in the world; and, in truth, his aggression had jeopardized every means of his existence. Only after years of treatment did we together understand that, behind the mask of hostility, lived a sensitive little boy who used his snarling, aggressive behavior as a practical defense against being overwhelmed by the world. He needed his hostility as a device for living; as a pseudo-ego, his only pride.

Some clinicians call such a case borderline schizophrenia; others, ultra-masochism. And when we ask what is at the root of such hostility, different students give various answers depending on their particular viewpoint and field of interest.

The biologist will say: his lack of tolerance toward stress is the result of hereditary structural anomalies. In animals we can study this relation between tolerance-capacity and hostility and aggression very well. In the epileptic fury—the worst clinical form of destructive hostility we know—man exhibits not merely a reaction to frustration but also suffers from an organic mismanagement of energy. Freud's concept of *destrudo* is somehow related to this anti-vitality principle and mismanagement of energy.

The therapist most oriented in early feeding frustrations of the child will say: see, this hostility is not real aggression, but a masochistic defense against oral incorporation, the fear of being eaten.

The psychologist most interested in toilet-training will show us in this case the need to ward off primary parental persecution with anal magic and defiance. As depicted in many old paintings, the anus becomes the dwelling of the devil.

Those who stick to the primacy of the Oedipus complex will explain that, beyond all, this patient is still symbolically killing his father and every comparable authority, his ex-wife included. Or they explain his aggression as a reaction-formation against his castration fear. Sometimes aggression replaces pure libido; sometimes it is the opprobrium of it

The more environmentally oriented student of social relations will give us insight into the manifold frustrations the man went through, inciting a vicious circle of new frustrations.

The existentialist will say, in philosophical terms, that people hate what they depend on, and that the more dependent people are, the more they hate. Man's hostility is the guilt of existing, his creativity the eternal rebellion against his creator.

The over-moralizing therapist will philosophize about hatred, hostility, and original sin, and will emphasize that the child has to learn to love those who frustrate him.

Those convinced of the conditioning effect of early infantile traumata will formulate that every hatred and hostility is primarily hating something in oneself; it is an abstract hatred directed toward the early magic introject, that is, the early fantasy about hostile figures settling in the child as nearly unconquerable prejudices.

Those who prefer to analyze the defense mechanisms as a therapeutic device see hostility and aggression as a frustration and disguise of infantile megalomania or as a pseudo-aggression covering up deeper-seated guilt and self-destructiveness. Others may speak of primary and secondary aggression, and we are all aware that man becomes enraged when he sees qualities in others he does not like in himself.

These are all metaphors, sometimes giving clarification, sometimes obscuring the individual peculiarities of each case.

I do not believe in a limiting definition and a single simple theory of hostility and aggression. Spinoza said: "*Omne determinatio est negatio.*" Any definition is a limitation. We always have to take into account many factors, biological and energetic factors included. Sometimes there is an overflow of energy, sometimes a lack of energy that may let people act with hostility.

But most important of all is that hostility and aggression represent the expression of a complicated human relationship. It often depends on what the mate, or the environment, or the culture, is used to accepting as hostile. When a child does not get affection, it prefers hostility as a paradoxical tie. We may also react hostilely to the strange and unknown.

The initial struggle between man and his fellow-man for dominance and submission is solved in different ways. This is the horizontal relationship between men. Self-assertion and rebellion constitute (or did) a Western ideal, but are looked upon as hostile in Eastern culture.

Yet, hostility is also determined by hidden vertical relationships in which the person reacts differently on different levels of his psyche, and in which one part of him may act in ways hostile and destructive toward the other part. We see this, for instance, in psychosomatic diseases. A hostile threat is usually more a symbolic trigger than a reality danger. And we see this especially in the sexual act, where taboo and non-understood guilt come into play—and may convert bodily pleasure into feelings of hostility.

For an example of this, I can point to an outwardly peaceful and harmonious couple, both of whom were active in the pacifist movement. Both husband and wife were ardent students of psychology and both were always holding hands; they trembled when the words hostility and aggression were heard. The wife, however, was the dominant idealist.

The marriage went on the rocks when she discovered that her husband had an additional homosexual marriage Their harmony proved to have been fraudulent. Their mutual love had been a mask. Their sexual encounters had been an unconscious attempt at mutual destruction. This, by the way, is not unusual. There is in our disturbed epoch much fornication born of hostility rather than love.

Sublimation of aggression

Primary normal aggression in man is a form of energy in the service of self-assertion, which, once aroused, must have some release. The basis for the development of many of our culture patterns has been man's ability to transfer some of this energy from defensive and destructive channels to constructive, unaggressive ones. The study of children reveals that they, as well as adults, can successfully transform and sublimate their aggressive and destructive tendencies into creative work, play and sports They can learn to endure frustrations and to increase their frustration-tolerance, if the original surplus energy can be displaced to a more socially acceptable aim. This displacement of aggressive energy is a symbolic and unconscious process.

After the world wars, when, for a short time, men were more consciously aware that they were no longer master of their unleashed drives, there was an increased tendency to engage in sports and dancing and other forms of mass-ecstasy and mass-release. However, the sensationalism of big sporting events did not aid materially in sublimating the distorted aggressiveness set free or accumulated during the war years. The aggression of the spectators often stimulated the aggression of the contestants, and unbridled ambition gradually overcame the idea of fair sportsmanship.

Repression of aggression

Let us tentatively accept normal aggression as a primary adaptive force necessary for the defense of life. It is the normal tool of self-assertive defense. As I have pointed out before, this source of energy does not relinquish its hold or disappear when it is not used after its initial arousal and mobilization. It merely goes beneath the surface, where its energy may be used in a system of mental and physical defense reactions. However, destructive magic fantasies may add secondary neurotic aggressiveness to those latent forces

Sometimes, as a result of such repressed neurotic aggression and a squandered mobilization of forces, there may emerge a less vital personality, with less "organic" adaptivity and adjustment to its environment. The human being who finds no outlet for his imaginary hatred now has to defend himself against his artificially-created fantasy enemies by other means: through delayed hypercharged anticipation; through hate, bitterness, guilt, melancholy, rebellion, cruelty. Such an individual may impose rigid inhibitions on his actual desires in the service of his hypercharged anticipation of hostility; the consequent sense of frustration may cause such self-hatred that the aggressive and destructive energy may be turned from the outside world toward the inner self.

When man, and especially man's conscience, can no longer endure the burden and tension of repressed aggression and hostility, he either explodes toward his fellow being under the guise of some justification, or he destroys himself. He is constantly on the alert and easily provoked. In this situation, the slaying of the foe or the slaying of the self may become one and the same act in the individual's mind. In one upheaval and outburst, he may liberate himself from the bonds of civilization by unchecked attack or by suicide. We find such a form of destructive amok in some psychotic people.

What we usually call hatred and hostility are different from the normal self-assertive aggression. They are hypercharged fantasy-products, mixed with reactions to frustration of the normal defenses, and they form a system of intense anticipation of increased discharge in the future. Numerous destructive fantasies can be involved.

If parents could differentiate between normal, healthy self-assertion in their children and neurotic pseudo-aggression, they could turn the child's surplus energy into productive and creative attitudes toward life, rather than repressing it and causing irreparable damage to the child's personality.

Scapegoatism and projection

One of the main defense reactions which man has devised to relieve himself of the burden of repressed aggression is the mechanism of projecting evil motivations onto an imaginary enemy. He transfers and displaces his own evil and destructive thoughts onto a scapegoat. He can turn the full force of all his repressed aggressiveness toward this fantasy-creation, the scapegoat, and can justify and exonerate himself for his cruelty. Bergler calls this passive fantasy-product man's "injustice-collecting mechanism," leading to many masochistic and sadistic actions and a continual provocation of new injustices to prove that the world is unfair and one's hatred justified.

In an earlier epoch of civilization the black sheep was sent into the desert burdened with the collective guilt and collective evil of the primitive community, and loaded with all kinds of magic fantasies. It was believed that by offering this "scapegoat" to the gods, the group guilt was absolved and the group soul cleansed of its evil intentions.

When the king appeared in history, he had to be made free of the sin of murder and destruction. He was anointed. As a symbol of the king's purification, the ceremony of the old offering of the blood of a scapegoat was repeated on the day of his enthronement.

As a result of this magic ritual of purification—heaping all sin and evil on the scapegoat—the king and leader reached a magic position very near to the gods At one time in history the offering of a human sacrifice made the leader and king free of sin; later, during the Middle Ages, as a reminiscence of this human offering, criminals or traitors were publicly executed on the day of the enthronement of the king In modern times we find a similar purifying strategy followed in a paradoxical way: the king pardons a group of criminals on the way to his coronation, reversing the procedure by the forgiveness of fellow sinners Our President and governors derive their right of pardon from this age-old ritual.

As Freud teaches us so significantly, man retains toward a king or father-figure an ambivalent attitude comprised both of extreme love and veneration, and extreme hate and envy.

There was little emotional reaction or mourning in Germany when Hitler died. Both divine honor and less-conscious fanatical murder-wishes had been projected onto him by his followers simultaneously. His command justified the criminal acts of the Storm Troopers. Yet, the Germans' displaced feelings of hatred —from Hitler toward the Jews—had temporarily been more satisfying because these feelings could be acted upon and could help to release their bitterness immediately. To the German people, every Jew represented both an atom of inner hatred and hatred of the Fuehrer. There was no ambivalence about this displaced feeling. The Germans were able to hate the Jews wholeheartedly and to vent upon them all their pent-up hostility. They needed this hatred to make "love" toward the Fuehrer possible. All people need this form of partial mental split in order to become ruthless, cruel beings. They are willing to forget the horrors —the martyrdom of defenseless victims—to exonerate themselves of guilt. People need criminals in order not to despair about their own little crimes

Man's savage past lies close behind him. It is perhaps a miracle that such bestial symptoms as those displayed by the Nazis do not reveal themselves more often. Civilized man is a rather young being in the history of mankind. We know that mankind has existed on earth more than 200,000 years, but only the last 6,000 years show patterns of progressive civilization. During all of history, human beings have tried to discard civilization because their innate bestial instincts moved them so strongly; yet, at the same time, they have attempted to subdue these animal instincts. The contradiction in these attitudes has resulted in continuous inner conflict. Men have found it simpler to project their faults and sins and suspicions onto others—and blame them—than to fight out their inner battles with their own conscience. They search for a scapegoat in an attempt to justify their own anti-social thoughts and actions. We may even say that modern "civilization," with its technically improved communications, finds it easier now to transfer suspicion onto others and to discriminate against scapegoats in order to unleash the most destructive aggressions towards groups of fellow beings.

Various kinds of racial and group prejudice satisfy a kind of mass resentment and mass hate After every war there is something to resent, so scapegoats and black sheep are still in demand. One has only to accuse—without proof—and the scapegoat is born. The persecuted is always guilty. People like to build up their animosities for others. "Not we, but they!"

—II—

A war is fought under the catchwords, "liberty" and "democracy," for "human rights" and "humanity." The Nazis used these same slogans. Six million people were burned to death like rats because of racial fiction and infantile destructive fantasy. The world will not forget these victims. Because they were victims, they will be inwardly judged guilty, for the world doesn't want to accept the blame for letting such horrors occur. The human mind always argues along the lines of weakest resistance. For the psychologist, this is proof of the dangerous, omnipotent destructive fantasies of frustrated children. Machine guns in mature hands led by infantile fantasies!

Werewolves and colored shirts

In addition to scapegoatism, man has devised other forms of magic strategy to relieve himself of his burden of hatred and to "purify" himself of inner guilt. One is the fantasy of becoming a werewolf. Through this ancient magic device man virtually changes himself into a wild beast, and by so doing purifies himself from sin. He creeps into a wolfskin, or a brown shirt, or even a military uniform and so identifies himself in his own imagination with a savage warrior or beast· a werewolf. The skin may be real or imaginary, but the man who is possessed by the werewolf delusion permits himself to unleash, without inhibition, all his bestial brutishness, and—like the historic "werewolves" of the Middle Ages—feels free of moral guilt. In our modern admiration for the uniform, we find traces of this old werewolf delusion.

Even fanatical ideas serve the same magic disguise. Man can be possessed by religious fanaticism or racial discrimination to justify his inner need for destructive behavior. The Germans of the twentieth century reached the peak of scapegoatism and the werewolf delusion in their persecution of the Jews.

The Nazi beast was the human beast

People nearly always speak in terms of pathology when trying to give an interpretation of brute Nazi behavior. "Those crimes could only have been committed by insane beings," they say, if they have any realization at all of what happened in the concentration camps of Europe. They abhor the ideas that such behavior could belong to the normal patterns of human behavior.

Were the butchers from Auschwitz and Belsen-Bergen and Dachau morally insane? Did they belong to that type of innate psychopath without normal development of conscience? We now have enough evidence to say no. Perhaps there were a few morbid types who incited others to act more morbidly, but, in general, the butchers were ordinary German people, mentally changed by the experience of living under the morbid hypnosis instilled by a totalitarian state.

When I was a prisoner, a very intelligent Nazi officer attempted to justify what the Nazis were doing. His manner was quite friendly, a trick often used by the Nazis to break the defiant silence of their prisoners. He was fully aware, he told me, of the human miseries, the atrocities, the horrible regression in German behavior. But he justified Nazi techniques by referring to examples of the same type of behavior in the Allied countries. He developed for me a pessimistic philosophy about the crudity of all human behavior—and how this hurt his tender soul! Such bestial behavior had been normal to mankind since the beginning of time, he insisted, and that was why he now was able to use such techniques for the good of the Fuehrer and the Fatherland, though inwardly he abhorred them.

I understood his attempt at self-justification and mental blackmail. Fortunately, I was able to escape his clutches before the principles of his "noble" dialectics turned into a more active torture; but from the moment of our conversation, I was better aware that the abnormal bestial behavior of the Germans belonged to possible human patterns, and that I could have done the same to this man under certain psychological pressures, while narcotizing my conscience.

We now have a large amount of diagnostical notes from persons, including psychologists, who lived inside German concentration camps These notes substantiate the theory that most Nazis were not abnormal psychopaths. "But," people still ask, "why did they never show pity for their victims? How would it be possible to behave in such a bestial way toward other human beings?" The answer is easily understandable to those who lived in the midst of the Nazi regime. Many Germans were systematically trained to release their pent-up hatred onto their different scapegoats—the Jews, the American capitalists, the Bolshevists, the Democrats—and to project all their frustrated wishes for vengeance upon them. The scapegoat is no longer considered a human being; he acquires the image of a devilish animal. We see this everywhere in the world where there is discrimination. For years the Germans were subjected to the suggestion. "Your enemy is a being without human rights . . ." They were hypnotized into becoming killers only. For them there was only one moral law, the raucous voice and the will of the Fuehrer.

"In the struggle for Nazi life you cannot use pity, culture or conscience." The Nazi youths were trained to repress all moral feelings, particularly where their "enemy" was concerned. Striving for a greater Third Reich and Valhalla, they were not permitted to show any emotional reaction. This was the only way in which they could develop the necessary blind spot for the suffering of their human scapegoats. They could beat children and women to death as we do mosquitos. The S. S. officers I interviewed lived, as it were, in an ideological hypnosis. In those interviews they gradually became aware of their crazy actions and some broke down under their guilt.

And what happened to the remnants of man's conscience? Instead of listening to their own personal conscience, people were trained to listen to an immense fanatical mass-delusion, the new German national conscience, the aggressive morale of the Third Reich. The collectivity, the state or community, was the condensation point for the destructive longings of the individuals. A collectivity can become aggressive more easily than an individual can. A collectivity also has more aggressive tendencies than the individual, because there are less inner hesitations of pro and con to overcome. Indeed, part of man's moral norms come from the collectivity, and the individual easily loses his sense of responsibility when the collectivity tells him to kill and murder. It is easier to hate and to be destructive in a collectivity because there is no individuality, no inner arbitrator, no inner judge, no fear of guilt or punishment.

The Nazi conscience praised, instead of punishing, the bestialities of its members, and most of the individuals did not feel uncomfortable when they themselves behaved in an utterly degrading manner toward their victims. The personal feelings of guilt, pity and conscience were safeguarded by the Nazis, for in their own private circles there was a complementary over-compensation of sentimentality, an exaggeration of feelings and emotions, a nearly hysterical pity for one another—or tremendous mutual hate.

The strategy of criminalization

From early youth the children in the Third Reich were imbued with the idea that the highest ideal was to die for Fuehrer and Reich; that the cause of all their troubles was, in Hitler's words, "their Jewish enemy, which they had never sought to harm, but which had tried to subdue and enslave the German people and which was responsible for all the misfortunes that had haunted Germany through many years." Every hour, every day, in every lesson, the children heard of death, hate, and human sacrifice. They were constantly injected with artificial hatred. They were impregnated with the idea of becoming passive instruments for the Reich, without personal will. The Reich thinks, the Reich feels, the Reich demands. In this way all personal conscience and responsibility were excluded and a national conscience was developed. The daily work school, the practical laboratory for criminalizing their minds, was the persecution of the guinea pigs, the Jews. Hitler once said that "you must teach your people to be brutes and to kill and to persecute, and then you have a firm grip on their minds and somehow as soldiers they cannot surrender any more."

In looking at German criminal behavior, it is wrong, therefore, to think in strict terms of pathology. The Nazi beast was the human beast whose behavior was shaped in a criminal mold by the fanatical Nazi ideology. What happened in Hitler's Germany was the result of political conditioning and training, a product of the Nazi system. The same can happen anywhere a dictatorial clique gets its "foot in the door." Nazism, Fascism, Soviet totalitarianism have shown us how far ultimate human regression can go in our civilized world, how, through mass training and mass contagion, it is possible in a short time to change completely the moral equipment of a nation.

The world is full of scapegoatism as a defense against the things man does not like to have happen and does not understand. And beyond this, man is always fighting against his cruel inner fantasies. The inconceivable, the greater thought, the other "it," all that goes above the comprehension of his mind or above the level of the group mind, he hates. One may use derogatory names such as "the international pluto-bolshevist" or "Amero-capitalist" and cry of threats to the security of the community or nation. Scapegoatism continues to satisfy the confused feelings and need for revenge in the immature human mind.

Every day people sacrifice their scapegoats on the altar of their guilt feelings and delusions.

The strategy of non-aggression

I once had an interview with Nehru on the strategy of non-aggression. We talked about the implications of the cold war and Gandhi's famous strategy against England, *satyagraha*, non-aggressive civil disobedience, and I asked him if he could acknowledge the existence of a subtle and rather dangerous ***mental*** form of aggression and hostility, often resulting in greater provocation of enemy or oppressor. He first wanted to brush off this delicate subject. Yet it is a well-known fact that the so-called peaceful, non-aggressive, passive resistant attitude may, quite paradoxically, arouse increased violent feelings in the other person. *Passive resistance works well only when the enemy adheres to the same ethical principles.* The British did not know how to cope with it because of their own subtle feelings of guilt.

Passivity and non-aggression are often falsely interpreted as mere defiance and passive sabotage by those who have no inkling of the moral values represented. Silence may arouse strange mental pressures in people and induce inner irritations that often weigh more heavily than the pain of aggressive bullets. The Nazis called the poker-faced noncommital equanimity of their tortured victims "physiognomic insubordination," and punished it very severely. They usually killed those haughty silent defiers immediately. They only tolerated meek faces and submissive characters. There is something in criticism and hostility—and the inner freedom to express them in words—that establishes part of man's self-confidence, because there is no fear of retaliation and aggressive discussion.

Nehru countered by saying that Gandhi had always emphasized that neither physical aggression nor spiritual hostility ever solve any problem. The very moment, however, that one's delusion of higher wisdom, one's strategy of restrained silence and unaggressive disobedience, provoke anger in the other fellow, some residual fear is bound to be communicated from the silent to the angry man.

Here, indeed, Nehru touched an important psychological point. Only strong personalities are able to use spiritual weapons, though they can temporarily induce other people to act according to the same courageous ethos.

The Prime Minister told me proudly that during the years of rebellion against Great Britain in India's struggle for independence, no Englishman was ever personally in danger of being physically attacked.

Gandhi always taught his disciples, Nehru continued: "Don't be afraid, don't be afraid."

How can people follow Gandhi's well-known method of *satyagraha* as a political tool, while unarmed and without rancor, but with fear in their hearts? The enemy knows how to shatter false courage. The worst of all dangers is the constant anticipation of new dangers. That is why Gandhi emphasized the great Oriental truth that wise men should have only few possessions. Luxury and possession of material wealth make people more afraid and vulnerable, because unobtrusively there is always the fear of losing their acquisitions.

Satyagraha and non-aggression require a high degree of ethos and a high morale of the population. As long as it is merely a subtle attempt to blackmail and burden the ethos and guilt of the enemy, there still is fear and aggression in oneself, and one often provokes the opposite. An eventual totalitarian invader would welcome such strategy of non-aggression. It saves him troops and he knows how to deal with it.

In talking with Nehru, I brought up the subject of the tremendous destructive passions that had been aroused, with murderous consequences, during the unreasonable conflict between Moslems and Hindus shortly after India regained independence. Nehru explained that here, too, fear, superstition and insecurity had been greater arousers of passionate hostility than political principles and well-aimed aggressive strategy.

Aggression, hate and fear

Aggression, hate, and fear belong together. The insecure individual who fears life and fears death feels himself free and great only when he can hate. Just as a dog attacks other dogs out of fear—my Scotty attacks only when he is on the leash and feels himself limited and frustrated—so man comes to hate. He grows to fear overt aggressiveness; he becomes too frightened to act. So passive hate becomes enough for him.

When free energy and free expression are suppressed to the extent that man must use such inner defenses as the anti-social feelings of deep hatred, bitterness, cruelty (which are stored-up passivity and neurotic aggression) to relieve himself of the anxiety caused by this inner destructive force, he develops guilt feelings. And when his aggression is completely suppressed, all kinds of new fears may come to the fore, fears that may turn again into explosive aggression. Now fear has become a thrill and fascination. The new drive for danger and power, for the thrill of new turmoil, serves to disguise man's deeper fears. So man gets caught in a vicious circle of fear. Peace has become an empty boredom for him. He needs turmoil to escape fear.

After every war an intensified confusion of feelings exists. The foe has been beaten and killed, but this usually succeeds in implanting an unconscious feeling of guilt in the human heart. The postwar hangover and the new feelings of guilt demand a purifying ritual.

When the primitive warrior came back from the warpath, he was not allowed to enter his village until he had purified himself of his guilt, sometimes over a period of time. That rite was not merely an animalistic superstition, resulting from a simple feeling of guilt, but was the beginning of a strong ethical sensitiveness which is lost in our modern culture. The primitive killer, identifying his victim with his own father, mourned as a son over the slain one. In our modern society, we are less certain of our feelings of guilt, although we find these feelings buried in the war neuroses and battle panics of both veterans and civilians.

One soldier whom I treated for war neurosis had killed an

enemy soldier with a hand grenade and was compulsively forced to look at the man's papers. Then he looked up the address of the man's relatives. He kept imagining the sorrow he had caused them, and kept wondering what they were thinking. He could not rid himself of the idea that he should earn a living for these relatives of his victim.

His first therapist had ridiculed his moral compulsion and this had increased his fears and depression. But then we could finally bring back his great shock to similar destructive acts toward a sibling—he once had nearly killed his younger brother—and that gradually cleared up his great anxiety.

Ill-defined fear and guilt normally occur after every war and are quite different from the reality-fear manifested during the active period of battle and destruction. This may be due in part to the long years of real fear and suffering, but it primarily arises from man's hidden feelings of guilt, especially in the conquerors. When a soldier has been forced to loosen his moral bonds and has traveled the world hating, revenging and slaughtering, it is only natural for him to bear some form of guilt on his return to his home. The defeated enemy always had to pay a severe price for his foolhardiness, but the conquerors come home to celebrate the horror.

Primitive man was tormented by his conscience after he had killed his enemy, but he knew why his conscience bothered him. He understood his guilt, had no conflicts about being hero and murderer simultaneously, and had a ready-made ritual for admitting his guilt and cleansing himself of it. Often, the eating and incorporation of the slain enemy represented such an act of purification. The enemy's soul was united with the soul of the conqueror.

Modern man's conscience is much more complicated. It is hard for him to rid himself of guilt-feelings that are often not understood. He has too many official justifications for being a soldier-murderer. That is why there is a tremendous accumulation of unconscious guilt-feelings in the modern world. It is to extinguish their guilt that people unknowingly long for a new, but this time self-defeating, war and catastrophe. That is why the current atomic war of nerves—the cold war—is not psychologically sound. The cold war is apparently being waged on the theory that fear of another war and the atomic bomb's tremendous destruction will force mankind nearer to a productive plan for peace. We will see that insecure men actually prefer the discharge and destruction of war to the pent-up inner tensions of peace. Neurotic aggression is no self defense. It is a cruel fantasy asking for punishment and self-defeat. Such people say, and believe, that the idea of atomic destruction repels them, but unconsciously they may enjoy the magic image of the bomb's huge destructive power.

An armistice does not solve human aggression immediately, and the cold war keeps fears alive. War itself starts an inner chain-reaction of fear, aggression and the urge for destruction. It criminalizes mankind just as Hitler criminalized Germany. World War I was the beginning of the aggressive chain-reaction in mankind, and the unconscious "earthquake" is still going on.

The non-socialized aggressive tendencies of the human being can be reflected in individual crime. Repressed aggression must come to the fore, and crime is a form of protest against a society that has restricted man's release of passions. The criminal recognizes only the sovereignty of his drives, not the sovereignty of the community Often, he merely asks through his crime for punishment for internal tensions he can no longer bear.

Crime is also a regression to the inter-individual archaic war of primitive drives fortified by infantile fantasies. Through the ages law and justice have been able to limit crime enormously. People feel themselves rather well protected by the police against individual criminal aggression, yet, so far, they have established no guarantee against the international discharge of emotions in mass aggression.

Aggression and war

There is a direct relation between man's inner destructiveness and the accumulated mass aggression directed towards an outside enemy world. Some individuals can externalize all their urges for self-destruction into hate, revenge and the destruction of others. Comparable psychological processes take place in the social sphere. In a country with accumulated non-adjusted mutual aggression of groups of political systems, the internal aggressiveness can be discharged in rebellion, revolts, scapegoatism, or in a war against a common outside enemy. The Nazis, for instance, often came to the point of mutual annihilation. It nearly happened in 1934 on the "Night of the Long Knives."

Consequently, the strategy of the dictator is ever to play up the threat of a common enemy from outside in order to achieve the pseudo-unity of his country. Every country with unstable and aggressive inner relations is forced to wage such an outside war to discharge the inner aggression; otherwise internal revolution arises. Internal conflicts, internal aggression and rebellion inspire new wars. As Freud said: "Foreign wars are the price of internal instability."

—III—

The caveman has appeared once more and stands scowling outside his cave, club in hand, ready to defend himself against all dangers. Hunger, cold, his fellow man, even his own sons are his potential enemies. Being a modern civilized citizen as well as a savage, man has to face (in addition to external danger) innumerable internal dangers—dreams, doubts, fantasies, mysterious inner forces, good and evil spirits—which fill his soul with awe. Like his primitive brother, twentieth-century man is engaged in total war with the environment, but, unlike his primitive brother, he also finds that he is constantly at war with himself. Obsessed as he is by vague inner fears, he can find no real rest anywhere in the world; a secure material basis for his life has gone, dwindled away through a series of economic upheavals. The spiritual basis for his life has gradually been washed away by the advancing currents of mechanized science and fanatical ideologies. Even the air man breathes, and the sky to which he turns his eyes, are no longer safe, for the winds may carry poisonous gases, and the sky rains bombs. Treaties and promises are broken. Even the gods are changing under the impact of stronger fanatical suggestions.

Civilized man in our time is conscious of only two alternatives. he can defend himself against these innumerable dangers or he can submit passively to them. He evokes an ever-increasing amount of neurotic aggression and suspicion in an attempt to combat the ever-increasing dangers and frustrations. He cannot develop the potentialities of mind and body to the fullest for he is obliged to live always in a state of alert preparedness, though he often dreads to be aware of this.

What a price mankind pays for this premature sapping of its powers and for this constant burden of fear!

CHAPTER THREE

Prejudice, Our Daily Test

This chapter, while seemingly giving primary attention to anti-Semitism, simply uses one of the most frequently-studied forms of human prejudice as an example for *all* racial, religious and political bias.

Hitler-like exterminations of vast masses of people still take place today, though the prejudices appear with different names and new labels. Discrimination is always used as a tool of aggression and as a strategy of war in the service of pugnacious aims. The pretext of discrimination originated in man's perverted need to blame others for the conflicts he provokes himself. The solution of human discrimination—and mutual suspicion—is the core of the problem of political sanity in the world.

Prejudice, scapegoatism and discrimination are to the psychologist valuable gauges of latent inner tensions in individual or group. They tell him how much need there is in the person to blame others for conflicts and confusions living in the person's own mind.

Everywhere, where persecution and malediction of minorities is part of the potentate's strategy, we can be sure that he acts out an inner conflict without being aware that only insight and self-correction will be able to heal the feelings of uneasiness and anxiety in him.

The *need to blame others* as a sham-strategy to evade one's own involvement and responsibility starts very early in every child's life and grows, in mature beings, into those multifarious hate-complexes poisoning our world.

At the very time when German audiences were silently viewing the stage production of *The Diary of Anne Frank,* I was traveling around the world in order to gather more information about these most tragic of man's inner conflicts, prejudice and scapegoatism. The word "tragic" here is used to express the lack of awareness of dark inner drives urging man to commit deeds against his conscience. Those same German audiences lived twenty years earlier under the shattering delusion that the little girl, Anne, belonged to the most despicable outcasts in the world. All their hatred went out towards Anne's race, doomed to be taken to the gas chambers. But now that they relive the revelations made shortly before her death by this utterly sensitive, flowering soul, they feel a deep burning guilt as they ask themselves: "How could we do it? Why did we?" (There is cause for hope when we recognize how soon the imprinted mass-delusion of racial inferiority can disappear if a sense of political reality and the freedom to verify facts break through.)

During recent years, America has been going through an honest, open, legal battle to overcome deep-seated feelings of prejudice. The revelation of a tragic division of minds comes as a shock to the country. This straightforward battle for a solution is headlined in the world press in critical and cynical phrases. I experienced this even in those countries where the same problems of discrimination were found in far greater proportion. Yet there was a general reluctance to touch on the subject of local prejudice "You'd do better to look after your own Negro problem in America than to talk about our Pariahs!"

An author who treats such an emotionally tragic conflict had better tell his audience about his personal, emotional involvements and biases before trying to be objective through a perhaps disguised and sophisticated approach.

As a Dutchman, I lived at the crossroads of two principal currents of prejudice. In our schools we were educated together with Oriental children coming from Indonesia and with colored children, Africans from the West Indies. In our classes—where the author, Multatuli, with his glowing sense of freedom and racial quality, was celebrated as one of the noblest representatives of Dutch literature—any form of personal discrimination disappeared.

A more subtle current was the latent anti-Semitism (wrapped in glorified tolerance) that existed; to it I was doubly sensitive, because I was descended from both Jewish and non-Jewish ancestors. Though the presence of this form of discrimination was mostly denied in our overtly liberal and tolerant country, it sought out its own secret pathways because there is in everybody some need to condemn someone and to find some scapegoats. Every classroom has its scapegoats. If necessary, one can even be prejudiced against left-handed children.

How to approach the problem?

As a clinician, I look especially for the underlying personal motivations that impel man to hate and reject his fellow man. I am deeply conscious that a growing awareness of what prejudice and scapegoatism mean in the personal make-up of man—and how easily we all are dragged away by them—will help to overcome this socially disruptive phenomenon.

Several approaches are possible to the study of discrimination, prejudice and collective hatred. One could start with so-called objective scientific research. gathering questionnaires and becoming involved in the statistical validity of these methods. One could also limit oneself to a purely historical description of occurrences and facts. As a psychological clinician, however, I want to follow a clinical-descriptive method, in which a multiple approach to the subject of research is emphasized; and in which both objective and subjective aspects are involved, as they are in every observation. To the clinician, incidental history often is a better experiment, done by fate and nature, than reduction of facts in the laboratory or opinion poll. One may call this clinical method a purely ideographic or historic one—as opposed to the causal deductive method of natural science. For such clinical description, personal empathy and the knowledge of man's inner psychodynamics are needed.

The method of examining social phenomena from different angles has its own reason for existence; it represents the various views on discrimination and collective hatred looked at not only by method-biased students of psychology but looked at too by the victims, who are often perfectly willing to accept their fate and blame and slavery. (Many Southern slaves were unwilling to live the life of an independent individual after Emancipation.) Also, the inner self-justifications used by torturers and aggressors are just as important in the study of discrimination as is the scientific analysis of objective facts. This sado-masochistic aspect of prejudice is a nearly forgotten subject in psychology. There are so many facets of human prejudice and hatred!

Arguments and counterarguments usually do not prove the logic and objectivity of our reasons, but are often the secret partisans of human hostility and aggression. It is easy to provoke countercharges and to let them dominate our discussions It gives release of anger and pent-up tensions, yet at the loss of better understanding.

There exist quite a number of slogans, racial pretexts and clichés to stir up such anger. Just give a dog a bad name and beat him! Beat and persecute the rightists and the leftists! Beat the colonialists, beat the conservatives! Always give the scapegoat a bad name—that justifies killing him!

Our daily political language is full of such politically prejudiced invectives of a servile humiliating language that tends to strike at the opponent. An old Chinese proverb explains that government means the affairs of the majority in charge. Both Laotse and Confucius believed in the wretchedness of an opposing minority. They were not aware, however, that their ruling class—those few who proclaimed themselves to be in power—represented also a minority in a majority and that both, *wisdom* and *terror*, always come from a minority of political partisans able to transfer its feelings and ideas to the masses with the help of weapons, the police and mass-suggestion.

As Chief of the Psychological Department of the Netherlands Army during World War II, and later as High Commissioner of Welfare, I had the opportunity to investigate many people clinically: both the Nazi aggressors and those persecuted by them. Much of the material gathered here I gave in abbreviated form in short lectures during those days of war and stress. Yet, it needed time to ripen into a more concise clinical concept. In a recent lecture trip around the world I tried to gather more clinical data because I look at discrimination as the core of the problem of mental hygiene and of greater political sanity in our world. Nevertheless, I want to make use especially of my personal encounters with fanatical and racial discrimination to clarify other phenomena of individual hatred and collective hatred.

Prejudice as an emotional barometer of the collective psyche

Especially during periods of stress and war can we witness the instability of collective feelings. Even among friends and allies we recognize sudden changes in attitude, outbursts of mutual aggression and hatred. For this reason it is worthwhile to investigate such changes in an attempt to arrive at a more objective approach.

What makes a psychological analysis of the roots of discrimination and mass animosity so difficult is the fact that every judge of this question is, at the same time, in the dock himself—never free from the very feelings and prejudices he wishes to describe in an objective way. This difficulty becomes particularly obvious when we single out for investigation one of the oldest forms of collective hatred, group prejudice.

The Jews, for instance, have made notable contributions to psychological analysis as an instrument of knowledge, but also as a tool of intellectual self-defense against feelings of insecurity. The Jewish community naturally tends to employ this weapon as a means of both attack as well as defense. Giving a sophisticated name to the mean motives of your enemy is already catching him by a word. Every glorifier of the so-called "Aryan" virtues or white supremacy or other form of racial prejudice may, therefore, stigmatize a psychological search for truth as "decadent" or "Semitic" or "colorblind." He may know nothing about the so-called Semitic race or about the Mongol race or the Negroes and yet may hate them as the result of some collective suggestion and mental contamination from outside.

This fact of *not knowing*—and even the wish *not* to know—plays one of the most important roles in the inner process of bias and discrimination. It is characteristic of hatred, as of all strong emotions, that the person possessed by it tends to reject every rational and intellectual analysis and that he is irrevocably pushed into an irrational and uncontrollable mood despite appearances of seeming logic, secondary rationalizations and justifications. The hostile subject very emphatically does not want his hatred to be analyzed, or understood, or explained in terms of his personal background; for under such circumstances the reasons for his emotional agitation would collapse. A person accustomed to examining his emotions cannot hate in the same way as a man unaware of the blocked and distorted workings of his mind. The very feeling of hatred is always based on a very limited orientation about oneself. Every broadening of outlook reduces and checks it.

Psychiatry reveals that the irrationality of hatred is rooted in uncontrollable infantile feelings of resentment. Bias and prejudice is, therefore, suited to be just as much the infantile magic weapon of the persecuted and outcast group. They counter the aggressive deeds and misunderstood magic of their attackers with their counter magic. In their passive hatred, the victims accumulate endless destructive fantasies—the ecstasy of hatred—till the time ripens for their explosion and retaliation. In many racially persecuted groups strange mystic rituals develop in which they experience ecstatic liberation from their fears. Think, for instance, of the Voodoo ritual and the need to kill the enemy in effigy, thereby hoping that he will be really harmed.

Rational psychological explanations may be insufficient indeed if they are used as tools against those in the grip of such feelings. One cannot fight overt hatred and aggression with words and essays. A person acting in emotional upheaval is not open to reason. On the contrary, his reason is subordinate to his violent emotions and is merely used to find more misleading arguments His opponent's theory is already contemptuously dismissed before it is heard and weighed.

We cannot fight with arguments against hatred and prejudice Deeds and examples have to occur, people have to be educated to understand what it means to be prejudiced. Straightening out the hostility aroused by racial and cultural differences will be mankind's most vigorous mental battle in the years to come.

Many feelings of hatred and resentment aim specifically at the intellectual processes in man and at the intellectual's capacity for overcoming primitive and infantile feelings. They represent merely man's protest against cultural repression and restraint of primitive instincts. One fellow reproaches the other for the ease of his self-control. Consequently many a form of collective hatred is anti-intellectual by nature. The hidden tempestuous emotions are experienced as the enemies of the intellectual brakes. The primitive man in each of us hates the rational man who has subjugated the archaic animal drives from the past.

The Jewish problem is only one example in an array of national and interracial passions. It is, to speak logically, a pseudo-problem, which acts only as a façade to hide other forms of prejudice and collective hatred. Nevertheless, since it is such an old problem, and since Hitler magnified its actuality so greatly, it presents many aspects that may contribute to a better understanding of racial discrimination and collective hatred in general.

Again, can racial prejudice and discrimination be observed objectively? Or better, could it be possible that, as a result of intensified psychological research and useful spread of acquired insight, the feelings of the hater and the hated, with their common justification and passions, could be eliminated? In my opinion this belief in intellectual scientific enlightenment is Utopian. In every analysis of emotions one should take into account the fact that small causes can provoke and trigger off big effects. The deeper motives for a general outburst of hostility are often brought into play by apparently trivial incidents as, for instance, happened with the Sepoy rebellion in India in 1859. The rumor that the Mohammedan soldiers were given pigs' fat for the cleaning of their rifles—in conflict with their religious ritual—released their latent hatred against the occupying British forces.

The mechanically and carefully instrumented mass-murder of Jews by the Nazis can only be explained as an outlet for a complex of long-concealed frustrations, hatreds and aggressions.

For example, both the Nazis and the Jews considered themselves victims of a universal conspiracy of the rest of the world against the "chosen" superior peoples. Violent suspiciousness can arise out of the identical historical experience of "enforced" inferiority. Under such inner tension one readily wreaks one's vengeance on a powerless competitor in both inferiority and superiority feelings. The Jews could the better satisfy the Nazis' need for increased self-esteem by becoming the Nazis' guinea pigs for expressing sadistic aggression: Hitler even cynically said once that he should have to invent Jews if they had not been there. The persecution of the Jews was the only way to instill more criminal aggression in his boys, the S S.

This, of course, is only one of the manifold aspects. But the search for greater inner self-esteem plays a role in any form of racial prejudice.

In this search for inner self-esteem, a subtle and nonapparent bias can play a tremendous role. There exists in nearly all people subliminal discrimination taking the form of continuously looking down on others in order to boost their own egos. This human quality may gradually incite the more ardent and active forms of prejudice Such prejudice is evoked by the vanity of over-self-consciousness of those who don't yet realize that their inner self, their inner make up, is distilled from many outer influences. Nobody is completely himself. Everybody is molded by many influences

Self-government and self-control begin at home. I have so often met people who shout and cry for freedom and self-government, but cannot direct and govern themselves. Unwittingly they use the catchwords of independence and self-steering as a paradoxical defense against inner confusion and bewilderment.

In the same way, discrimination starts at home. Social stratification and discrimination are a way of human coexistence. Mothers and fathers unconsciously have their preferences among their children, based on subtle mental interactions and inequalities, and children have their biases on the basis of overt and repressed sibling rivalry.

Some of the unwritten rules at home and the written rules in society serve to overcome these natural inequalities inherent in loving and being loved. Justice serves gradually to replace preference and bias. However, take law and order away and even greater bias and stratification may take place. This is what we see now in many former colonial nations. Many of them live temporarily in a void full of mutual bias and prejudice and are searching for new self-limiting rules and laws. Now that their common hatred against the occupying ruler no longer has any foundation and no outlet, they make scapegoats of each other.

However, by merely describing outbursts of collective hatred and finding some faraway motive, we do not solve our methodological difficulties of how to reach an objective point of view. Every small detail of such a collective outburst may have special importance.

The Jews as a group presented many details which Nazi-hatred could seize upon as conscious or unconscious pretext. The Jews have given Germany outstanding men in the fields of arts and sciences. This fact inflamed latent hatred—for intellectual envy is hard to bear. Nobody wants to deem himself less intelligent than his fellow men; so this feeling of inferiority is easily rationalized into more hostile accusations. Accordingly the myth was fabricated that the Jews had penetrated German economy and constituted a sort of international conspiracy against German economy. However well one could prove statistically that this was untrue—just because latent anti-Semitism had barred the road for many German Jews—it only fortified the myth of Jewish conspiracy. Even in the unexpected anti-Negro riots in England some time ago, the myth of economic infiltration and rivalry played an important role.

The Jews, with their traditional sense of cosmopolitan and international justice, also reinforced the bitter feeling of injustice which the Germans wrongly believed they were made to endure after the First World War. This self-pitying injustice-collecting mechanism plays an important role in the outburst of racial prejudice. The Jews in their dignified acceptance and tolerance of dispersal and exile constituted a living reproach to a nation which had yet to learn the great wisdom of acceptance of injustice and defeat. Walter Rathenau, the Jewish Prime Minister who served shortly after World War I, was considered the economic savior of post-World War I Germany, but he was felled by one of the first bullets shot by organized anti-Semitism. Rathenau, the politician and philosopher, was not thought of by the deluded ones as a leader of Germany, but as the leader of a world conspiracy against Germany.

The meaning of self-hatred and masochism

In the psychological study of feelings of hatred and mass animosity in general, a number of specific questions present themselves. In order to trace the origin of mass prejudice and mass hatred, one has to compare individual emotions with the feelings of the masses.

It is interesting, with regard to our example of anti-Semitism, that one should find the same prejudices and discriminatory "anti-feelings" among the Jews themselves. The Jew—and I speak here especially of those who feel themselves in diaspora (exile)—also has anti-Semitic feelings, a curious self-hatred that can be partly explained by his chagrin and disappointment that his group is not considered any more as representing "the chosen people."

In psychotherapeutic analysis we nearly always find that nobody consciously wants to belong to a doomed minority. He despises the fact that he could not select his own nest in which to be born. The racial "mark" is not a voluntary decision, but something arbitrarily imprinted by fate. That is what deeply, though often unconsciously, irks many a Jew—that he is a Jew or considered to be a Jew. The Ashkenazim coming from Eastern Europe entertain feelings of resentment against the Sephardim coming from Spain and Portugal, the cultured Jew against the less educated, the Western-European toward the Eastern-European Jew. In the meantime they also developed a vocabulary of derogatory, magic vituperation towards Gentiles. However, their mutual hostile feeling was hardly ever so strong that it interfered with mutual social and philanthropic actions among the *Jews* as a whole. The common danger of racial persecution won out over their mutual antagonisms, increasing their solidarity. But now in Israel we hear about the strong tendency of ethnic stratification of the population with a renewal and revival of old latent prejudices. When no racial discrimination is possible, cultural and economic stratification and discrimination start.[1] Stratification and discrimination are part of the psychological reality of human coexistence. The problem is how to find the limiting checks and rules.

Various national differences play a role in these prejudices and mutual resentments. A certain masochistic trend belonging to the mentality of every persecuted man, an inclination to melancholia, a general philosophical acceptance of the inferior position, all these may exclude to a large extent the concept of a hurt "point d'honneur" or of combative, rebellious reactions to the treatment they suffered These formerly submissive attitudes in Jews have completely changed since Israel became a free self-assertive nation. As said before, however, the more universal human need for stratification and differentiation could better come out openly.

It is not surprising to learn that many Jews accepted their fate in Hitler's horror-camps passively, almost in a state of mental paralysis. This specific submissive attitude is partly connected with the tenets of their ancient religion, according to which their God is a hard father who punishes the biblical children severely.

But there is also another, more deeply-seated factor in people helping them to "enjoy" slavery and persecution. In my recent talks with the lower Hindu caste, the Pariahs, it was amazing to experience how they philosophically justified their inferior position. They, the untouchables, would not think of being touched themselves by the Brahmins. Many could only live at peace with their burden of discrimination by passively justifying their fate.

It is startling in gathering information about caste prejudice in Asia to find how hesitant people were to give adequate information about this most resilient of institutions. In Ceylon I saw, for instance, how among the personnel of a hotel subtle differences in caste were kept intact. The lower caste did not want to eat from the plates of the higher caste and vice versa.

The concept of caste is accepted as the law, *Dharma,* the divine fate one must obey. It is almost more than religion because it spells out better one's duties and prohibitions and one's conformation to old taboos. According to Hamdi Bey,[2] part of the caste system can be attributed to the non-united tribal society that India really is, with its 300-400 castes and sub-castes. Every member of another tribe is essentially a foreigner. First the priesthood (the late Brahmins) came out as a united caste system, and later the Aryan invaders and warriors. But the Brahmins remained the highest caste.

Important for our research, however, are the masochistic tendencies among the lower castes to accept and repeat the established pattern of rank-order as chickens do in the chicken coop. As a result, different degrees of "being human" developed. Bey tells us that in an aboriginal group in Northeast Bengal there exist 30 castes in a population of 300. Only through endogamy and inbreeding could the feeling of tribal identity be kept alive. It is all part of the ancestor-complex, that vertical relationship of man, that illusion about what man owes to the family tradition and family line. Democratic freedom gradually lifts people out of this totemistic participation and identification with the dead ancestors. This constant regard for ancestors leads people to feel unreasonable obligation to do things they don't believe in any longer, just to pacify the souls of the ancestors.

The Nazis tried to revive the same kind of ancestor delusions with their schemes of racial purity To the family group (and to the nation) one belongs by compulsion, not by free choice. The tribe and family require compulsory uniformity· unity and uniformity comprise the underlying aim of the tribe. At the same time, however, this demand arouses a host of ambivalent feelings towards the vertical family phalanx, towards siblings, cousins and friends. The loyalty to hereditary fictions of greater purity is one of the most offensive for human tolerance and good human relations.

Among orthodox Jews we can find comparable ancestor idolatry and beliefs in regard to traditions and taboos The fear of the threatening father and patriarch, and the resulting passivity, may have been part of this hereditary traditionalism and inheritance of prejudice. The fear of the tyrannical father makes the search for a scapegoat elsewhere necessary—in this case the search for a lower caste serving as a scapegoat for displaced hatred. The scapegoat and eternal enemy in this case represents the tyrannical father in effigy.

Of importance, again, is the fact that rigid family ties, and the Indian system of joint family possessions, hamper the individual development that wants to reach beyond the historical tradition, and asks for its proper sense and justice. Yet, assimilation of new habits disturbs and endangers the tribal inertia. Buddhism with its matriarchal emphasis was partially able to correct this offensive caste system.

As another example of self-chosen rejection and pariahship, I can mention the Ziganes and also the Rodyas of Ceylon. According to myth this last tribe is supposed to have been punished once —long ago—because of their rebellion against the king; that is why they became slaves and pariahs. Another myth traces their inferiority back to incestuous sins, also committed ages ago.

What is of importance for our purposes is that many Rodyas accepted their fate and hereditary punishment in a proud retreat and with a feeling of reserve and concomitant self-pity.

Man's lack of private opinion, and man's lack of zest to fight for it, lead people to stick to the prejudices to which they had formerly been subjected.

This brings us back again to the concept of a *masochistic* wish for discrimination, a factor so well studied in actual psychoanalysis. Because of unconscious guilt, sexual guilt, guilt about hidden incestuous feelings, Oedipal guilt, or because of a juvenile dependency need, the role of slavery, submission and scapegoatism is chosen and even preferred. I have seen women in my practice who made their husbands into real or imaginary brutes because they wanted to pout and to be treated unjustly.

Even in modern democratic Japan there remain remnants of a rejected caste, the "Burskunin" or "Eta"—humiliated untouchables who are by tradition forced to remain in the lower professions The government has tried to liberate them from their old ban, as the psychiatrist, Professor Muria, told me. For centuries the "Eta" were not even registered in any Japanese census as human beings Only since 1868 have they gradually been restored to full citizenship. But the impoverished gravediggers, trash and brass pickers, the butchers, the ragmen, scavengers, and tanners come from a long line having the same lowly-judged occupations.

Another form of Japanese discrimination is directed toward those who married foreigners and returned to the fatherland because of divorce or death of their husbands. Their family record, their mixture with the foreign race, eternally makes them secondary citizens according to actual Japanese law.

In a 1957 news story from India we could read how the ancient traditional discrimination gets mixed up with political violence. This case concerned the southern state of Madras. Here the majority of untouchables—the Haryans—maintained a regime of terror over the Maravars belonging to the lowest of the Hindu castes (peasants, laborers, artisans). This rivalry and mutual discrimination in the lower echelons of the persecuted is of tremendous importance for our subject.

Independent India has made efforts to shake off the caste system. Gandhi called the Pariahs especially the "children of God." At the moment various of those groups are feuding for political power. At least that is the justification for current eruptions of violence. In reality, the more deeply-seated hatred of discrimination has not been so organized and repressed that it could be checked by normal democratic procedures.

The Jews, as a weak minority, have always been forced to react to persecution by plunging into spiritual depth and mental isolation. In all dire affliction it appeared to them "that they personally mattered nothing to God, the father," that their personal suffering was only part of the universal suffering of the world. Every minority has to learn to tolerate and justify injustice the hard way. The resulting glorification of the past is only the gilded justification to make the discrimination and suffering more acceptable.

It is conceivable that without racial prejudice, persecution and anti-Semitism, neither the Jews nor the Jewish rites would have survived. Paradoxically speaking, the age-long persistence of the Jews is the result of anti-Semitism.

The melancholic and philosophical sense of humor of the persecuted changes, however, all too easily to a curious self-hatred and resentment against their own community whenever their own position grows stronger. Nearly every improvement of the Jewish situation has led to a decrease of religious devotion and to an increase in internal anti-Semitism and search for assimilation. Meanwhile, however, the fear of the Gentile, of the man from the other race, of the eternal persecutor, has repeatedly forced them back into greater mutual solidarity. It was a particular tragedy of the Jews that their confused sentiments toward their own more liberal co-religionists often acted as water on the mills of Gentile hostility and anti-Semitism. The battle over Uriel Acosta and Spinoza in seventeenth-century Holland made the surrounding Gentile community more aware of this exotic religious enclave. Yet, we may also explain the hostility toward the Gentiles as a strategic battle of the rabbis against assimilation, fusion and decline of their group.

Racialism and discrimination as pretext

When people feel and are actually inferior, they can at least boast about their ancestors, about whom usually not so much is really known. There is a tremendous need to dig in the past to justify today, although I certainly don't want to offer so simple an explanation of the delusion of hereditary grandeur. Much of this delusion is rooted in ancient, tribal relationships and the strong vertical family ties which have already been mentioned. Our minds are molded and hardened in age-old patterns of thinking. It is important to recognize that the pretext of discrimination is used over and over again the moment one's own life is felt to be inferior. The scapegoat is the receiver of the displaced tension and aggression every molding to uniformity in the group arouses in us.

The eternal scapegoat

Let us try to find out more about the general concept of the scapegoat. Some examples of such consistent rivalry are even discernible in the animal kingdom. There, too, we see a continual fight for power as soon as animals live in groups. After a period of chaotic struggle, a certain hierarchy and stratification is instinctually set up. The strongest animal is the leader and he keeps that place until, in a new incidental fight or during general turmoil, he may lose the fascination engendered by his former victory and strength. In chicken-coops we speak of the *pecking-order*. Everyone waits his turn to peck his grain, depending on the order of power. The existence of this gradation and order of power and strength means that the feeblest animal becomes the last one in the conquest for food. He is the outsider, the "black sheep" among the chickens, he is only tolerated by the flock for his ability to receive all the beatings. The problem of suffering minorities in the animal kingdom is already a million years old. Eat or be eaten.

As soon as humans come together, the battle for power, precedence and rank-order also takes place, but it occurs in a more subtle way. Who is the most dominant one among us, who the meekest and more submissive? Biologically, it is known that in cases of mammals when the first food-seeking behavior gets disturbed or frustrated, a more permanently submissive attitude in the pecking-order may be conditioned. In clinical terms we may say that the initially rejected animal becomes a lastingly submissive animal that sticks to its pattern of rejection.

However, modern man in all his suppressed primitivity is not able to exercise his ancient blood-magic and revenge on the weak scapegoat without using political justification and fine-sounding theoretical distortion of thought. He cannot say, "I want to drink blood to become stronger myself." He cannot directly offer his scapegoats to the man-eating idols. He needs an "idealistic" philosophy, such as the Nazis had, to make his distorted cannibalism more acceptable. Or, he needs a reasonable mythology to cover his deep-seated guilt.

At the end of the Second World War, Hitler tried to make use of such an age-old myth to make the German youth more bloodthirsty. He and his hangmen started the werewolf movement, using old magic tales of werewolves in order to let the Hitler Youth identify with the cruel wolf and uninhibited animal in man. Only when man dreams that he is an aggressive wolf, and is unconsciously convinced of this, does he allow himself to be as ruthlessly aggressive as those animals. From that point on he is allowed to be cruel and without remorse. Effective propaganda can suggest and persuade people to become ruthless killers, caught in the "blood and soil" myth.

In order to keep up that old delusion of guiltless destructivity, cruelty and aggression, modern man needs some illusion of werewolves and scapegoats so that he may enjoy his untamed animal passion and drives. He is continually on the lookout for the eternal enemy. At least he has to send somebody into the desert or into the gas chamber or into racial segregation—someone who epitomizes his inner guilt and fear and moral uneasiness. He has to scold about the Jews and to spit at Negroes or other so-called inferior beings. Man must project onto others—on fictitious enemies—what he cannot tolerate inside his own psyche. He must cultivate prejudice toward others in order to tolerate himself. He must humiliate somebody else because once in his youth he felt weak and humiliated himself.

Scapegoatism is a universal defense against inner weakness; it is universal because once we all were babies and weak and dominated by others.

The roots of individual hatred and hostility

Where in the individual shall we seek for the roots of hatred and hostility? What are the origins of this violent urge to destroy one's fellow man or oneself? Hatred, death-wishes, guilt, fear, aggressiveness and sadism belong together. They are among the most primitive reactions of the individual to painful, dangerous stimuli. However, one should not consider this hostility as being of an entirely negative nature. Hatred is not merely repulsion and rejection, it wants more, it wants (in its original biological drive) to destroy *and* to devour. "Eat or be eaten" is the law of the jungle! It is connected with the primitive drive especially of the carnivorous animals of uniting with and incorporating what one fears and yet desires. Every psychologist who has witnessed mob violence, racial violence or lynching, must be aware how the deeply repressed cannibalistic tendencies come to the fore. Mostly it is observed taking the form of verbal expression, though from time to time real cannibalism occurs In Nazi camps lamps were made from the skins of Nazi victims.

Many a so-called "love" relationship when broken off may be converted into hatred because the hidden counterpart, the primitive urge to destruction and incorporation, remains.

Hatred and hostility belong to the fundamental struggle for life, and are connected with the fear of isolation from those members of the family or in-groups we do not have to hate In all probability, people were either friends or enemies in primitive times, according to the pattern of mutual love and trust in the family. Even the word *hostile* originally had a polar meaning as we find it back in the other derivative. *host.*

A friend, when he is expelled from the group, may suddenly become a foe. These initial attitudes are fostered in the family group and fortified a thousandfold by tribal habits and customs. Just as in animal groups the stranger or outsider is picked on or driven away, so the human outsider will be shunned and expelled from human societies still living in a primitive stage of mutual distrust.

Another of the deep roots of hate lies in the ambivalence, the inner contradictions inherent in the instincts of life. Every adaptation to reality starts with vacillating feelings—that is to say, the instinctual drive can be gratified by contrasting influences Every instinct, in order to grow up and reach mature fulfillment, fluctuates between abstinence, the pleasure of gratification and the pain of over-gratification. Every gratification entails lust and love; every over-satisfaction of the drive entails hatred against the object that helped to attain the loss-of-desire feeling. Through satiety and over-satisfaction, pleasure is turned into displeasure and revulsion.

Let us look at the earliest of instinctual gratifications of taking food. The pleasure-bringing stimulus-object (e.g., food) at first is incorporated with gratification; but in a later phase, after, for instance, enforced feeding by frustrated parents and the resulting "over-satisfaction," this pleasure may change into a paradoxical response such as "hatred" or "disgust." This is what we realize may sometimes happen in the genesis of the stomach ulcer. The once beloved food becomes the enemy. The combination of pleasure and anxiety produce a paradoxical reaction.

Only cultivated, well-measured gratification and pleasure do *not* bring about that transformation of appetite into revulsion. The whole set of cultural brakes and restrictions arms itself, as it were, against the change of positive into negative feelings and teaches us to choose the wisdom of moderation. Culinary rites plead for restrictive reasonableness. Alas, modern advertising promotes unrestricted chewing and gobbling, thus creating a new problem of overeating.

The same restraint and cultural moderation is true for the gratification of sexual instincts: otherwise love and hate come too near to alternating with each other. The hunt for continual orgasm and sexual satiety, for instance, may produce the most paradoxical aggressive reactions. The modern cult of over-gratification of sex play and precocious initiation calls forth revived ambivalent feelings between the sexes.

It is the task of civilization to put a reasonable brake on instincts and their need for hasty fulfillment and to harmonize them into a more stable fulfillment. At the same time, however, on a different level of the psyche, there arises a deep resentment toward those very cultural restraints. The limited capacity of cultured man to delay, inhibit, and frustrate instinctual gratification, though leading ultimately to a higher, cultivated pleasure and sublimated ecstasy, may make for greater instability of his inner life. Without tolerance—without the capacity to bear frustration and injustice—a man cannot adapt himself to our society.

The instinctive hatred toward restraint can cut through all cultural brakes; and then, in one mighty upheaval, the primitive human "animal" in man bursts out and falls upon its prey, again to devour it.

In sexual play, above all, the harmony of the various feelings is very unstable. Basic "libido" has in every cultured society been transformed into a more refined game of erotic play and physical love. But sexual "love" can easily change into hatred, after the erotic tensions have been relieved too easily, and particularly if the gap between the cultural level of the mates and the level of instinctual gratification is wide. We see this so often in the fragile relation between the client and the prostitute. A number of American soldiers from puritanical backgrounds sustained an acute psychotic breakdown when they arrived in a country of a different race and where sexual gratification as an age-old ritual was so easily obtainable with so much lovely dedication. After their orgasm they lived in a void filled with guilt and strangeness. They were not aware of the sudden upsurge—as they explained to me—of hostility toward themselves.

Hatred always means lost love. The hatred against cultural inhibition and restraint, as well as the deep inner fear of one's own uninhibited actions, may be alluded and projected onto the love-object. The converted physical "love" and the provoked psychic aggression can work together to destroy the beloved. The pathological extreme of this hostile situation logically leads to sexual murder. This libidinous, primitive form of hatred—the primitive wish to eat and incorporate the beloved mate—is unconsciously contained in every kind of racial hatred and prejudice. It is the urge to destroy the object or person through which one has satisfied—albeit only in fantasy—one's uninhibited instincts The Nazis had a symbolic word for this magic destructive idea. They called it the "Blutkit," the bloody glue that kept their S. S. men together in their "man-devouring" clan. Once a Jew was slain, more scapegoats had to be killed, to keep the idea alive of living beyond the normal moral commitments. The girls first had to be used sexually by Hitler's boys before they were to be offered to his Moloch, the gas oven.

But other primitive fantasies are combined with the sex act. There also remains in people, especially in the male, a primitive fear of having to perish after the moment of greatest instinctual enjoyment. It is perhaps to be explained as a biological remnant of death occurring immediately after copulation such as happens in the insect world From dreams we realize that neurotic males still have the primitive fear of being eaten and incorporated by the female in the sex act. From the moment that inner fantasy becomes too real, the circle of fear and hatred and murder is completed.

It is the unknown hatred and urge to destruction that make human sex relations persist even after love and Eros have ceased to exist. Often more sexual union is born of hate and aggression than out of love.

Why these meditations about sex? Because in every racial prejudice confused feelings of sexual attraction and sexual taboo play a role. "I don't want my daughter to marry a Negro," is often expressed by many a father as justification of his racial hatred. But in so saying he only expresses some of his own repressed incestuous desires, displaced towards the scapegoat. Hitler accused the Jews of the most horrible sexual crimes. Such fantasies had to come up in a man who was himself impotent and sexless.

Every hatred is also connected with man's innate suicidal thoughts, that is, with self-hatred. In everybody there lives the mystic idea that he, though he did not give life to himself, has the magic power to undo his parents' (and God's) creation. That is why there always lives in the suicidal thought the idea of resentment toward the creator, the parent or the leader.

The "enemy" to be killed in the rite of discrimination often serves as a screen onto which the persecutor projects his self-destructive feelings. The enemy from without is the scapegoat for the enemy within. This explains the peculiar emotional tie always present between hater and hated, between the murderer and his victim. This fact of subtle mutual relationship between the persecuted and the persecutor becomes even more clear in the process of menticide and brainwashing. The inquisitor and his victim form a team wherein mutual guilt and hatred try to resolve themselves, though the brainwashee usually goes to the gallows. Yet it often occurred that his judge and inquisitor followed him rather soon, being brainwashed himself and brought to submission by a new inquisitor, his successor to the procedure. When the hater has conquered and slain his foe, he has vicariously destroyed something inside himself. Consequently he may become depressed and burdened with feelings of guilt and hatred toward himself Such hatred may become dangerous for the aggressor, who feels "eaten up" internally because he identifies more and more with the victims who *were* virtually "eaten up." Instead of feeling satisfied, a kind of emptiness develops in him that continuously consumes a surplus of energy and asks for new prey, new persecutions, new killings.

Hatred and fear belong very closely together. The insecure individual with a fear of the complications of life and a fear of the finality of death feels relieved if he can hate and give vent to his pent-up aggressiveness. Just as primitive man in panic runs amok in order to destroy, so does cultured man hate with an endless yearning for destruction. Hatred and hostility break the unbearable tension of fear. Cultured man does not even need overt aggressiveness; it is sufficient for him to destroy, mentally—in fantasy—with endless cold hatred.

Racial prejudice often is a collective murderous fantasy of this kind. Hatred gives man new social status among all those who share his feelings, and a feeling of magic power. The hater lives in a constant inner ecstasy. Even a pathological idiot assumes a pseudo-personality when he preaches hate and destruction. Several egoless patients of mine became (in their own estimation) new personalities when the Nazis, who occupied their homeland, gave them the opportunity to feel real hatred. The reality hatred cured them of their obsessive defenses against their inner hostility.

Even a vague inner nagging about one's own guilt may result in redoubled hatred toward those who are the target of one's aggression Apparently, the unconscious feelings of guilt, particularly if they meet with kindness or submissiveness on the part of the victim, often reinforce the hatred. This psychological paradox plays an important part in the psychology of passive resistance and non-aggression. Especially when the aggressor doesn't share the same ethos, he increases his hate and self-justification because he explains his opponent only in terms of haughtiness and intellectual superiority. Thus, aggressive feelings, destructive thinking and inner justifications revolve in a vicious circle, hatred and guilt keep renewing each other deep down in the psyche until finally there may come a murderous outburst. This partly explains why Gandhi was murdered.

One's own uncomprehended sense of guilt leads to projecting guilt and blame and horror onto the fantasied enemy. That is why the eternal scapegoats are often hated more than ever, because of their very martyrdom. They appeal to man's conscience and guilt, and guilt is so difficult to bear.

It is a grave crime, indeed, to have been murdered and persecuted! As a rule, guilt is projected onto the victim rather than onto the persecuting criminal. Ironically enough, just as in primitive society, the Jews of Nazi Germany were slain, as it were, in the obsequies of their masters.

The eternal misanthrope

The man-hater or misanthrope is not a rare phenomenon. He is disgusted with himself and his world. He projects his fear of death and the injury done to his self-love on all men. The misanthrope really wants to torture himself inwardly and pile up injustice upon injustice. But instead he is often forced to torture other people because nobody wants to commiserate and to wallow with him in self-pity. Therefore, he destroys, he petrifies, as it were, free, spontaneous life, by his breath of death. His only concern is to recapture high status for his own ego. He cannot do it all by himself. He looks for it in others and wrings it from them. Out of a sense of guilt he sometimes showers them with gifts, he compels them to adore him, he flatters them. His unsuspected life's policy, however, is to derive pleasure from self-torture and from the torture of others, and in this way to increase his self-prestige by accusing the world of having bereft him in his early childhood. Overcome by jealousy he anxiously watches any warmhearted relation of a fellow-being with a third person. On the other hand, he also plays a role of the ethical flirt, the preaching narcissist. But his own mind is crying out for human appreciation, which it cannot win.

Misanthropes will be found on many levels of society. Driven by their sense of guilt, they are the pseudo-innovators of humanity, the dogmatic fanatical maniacs—as Hitler was—through whom the world is in danger of perishing. They will indulge in their prestige-policy everywhere. When in trouble, they become softhearted and cry bitterly over defeat, but with crocodile tears.

They may hide their aggressiveness behind an ethical façade. And they hate with an endless hatred—to protect themselves against the fear of rejection by their fellow-beings. Their hatred is nothing but an attempted protection against the continuous fear of isolation; actually they yearn for human sympathy, just as the Nazis did.

Collective hatred

Politically, hatred is important because it is such a tremendously contagious feeling. Common regression toward hatred is much more easily aroused in people than the progression toward mutual affection and love. Collective hatred especially can be easily aroused, while the individual is more inclined to resist his private hatreds. Individual man unwittingly learns to reflect upon his own feelings, and this self-reflective analysis often checks his private hostility. By contrast, no self-account needs to be given of collective feelings induced and provoked by the community. In the masses man is an anonymous non-responsible individual. This difference in self-reflection between the individual and the collective emotions is intensified by present-day education. Man is taught little about his responsibility for his own emotions and thoughts. "Thoughts are toll-free," as the saying goes; what smoulders inside the people does not harm one's fellow-beings, many people think. Thus man has never learned to be responsible for his feelings and for those he inadvertently arouses in others. He is seldom taught to resist being carried away by collective emotions. The growing emphasis on cold war, mass-propaganda and advertising makes mankind even more vulnerable to collective persuasion and collective emotions.

Here, then, lies one of the social roots of hatred. Man's growing vulnerability to mental contagion and psychic mass-infection —and his unawareness of this increased vulnerability!—are evident. Paradoxically, the surrender to mental mass-contagion is often associated with an intellectual fear of being carried away by the group, of losing one's individuality. People struggle with it without knowing what to fight against. Yet the means of mass-communication have been so coercive that hardly anyone is aware any more how much the official headline of the day acts on him.

A collectivity can hate by counting on no more than the general need for anonymity, depersonalization and common regression of its members. Mob violence often means only the aggressive ecstasy of anonymity. Every individual in the group is insidiously forced to identify himself with the collectivity; this psychic process of willy-nilly enforced common participation easily evokes latent personal hatred in each, and collective hatred in all. Therefore, the crowd and the masses can easily be roused to all kinds of violence and cruelty much more readily than the individual. Goebbels manipulated easily-aroused mass-feeling with extraordinary efficiency as chief of Hitler's propaganda department. He characterized his task as "to organize hatred and suspicion, to get the masses of men on the march—all with icy-cold calculation." Many modern propagandists of discrimination and racialism do the same but are not so aware of their venomous strategy.

Collective hatred is aroused with particular ease when the mental horizon of the group is narrow, and contact and communication with other groups impossible or forbidden; in that case people are all the more susceptible to inbred mass suggestion. Every feeling of isolation, of personal impotence, of being in a hostile environment, makes a man easily inflammable by suggested hatred. Were we to study mental infection, we would see that it is the induced common regression to an infantile primitive state that makes people so vulnerable to barbaric seduction.

Sexual distortion, as we've noted, plays a part, too. In the Nazi circles the Jew was looked upon—at least in their propaganda stunts—as sexually more lascivious, superficially explained as a result of his southern Semitic descent. And the same sexual myth of racial prowess is now told about Negroes. In reality, we find even more libidinal frustrations among the American Negro —possibly as a result of their socially inferior position. Clinically this shows in many complaints about impotence and frigidity. The cause of this inflammatory accusation is that people project the frustration of their own erotic desires upon the scapegoat. They externalize their own inner troubles. The scapegoat is always blamed for being more exotic in his instincts and needs. In the same distorted way the southern type of woman is often regarded as a more desirable love-object by frustrated northern Europeans.

These very sexual justifications and distortions are unbearable, however, to man now that he is frustrated by so many cultural brakes. He revolts against this inner tension, apparently for sacred ascetic reasons and for the purity of his own habits; he is in fact rejecting his own frustrated instinctual drives. Thus his unresolved lust and jealousy are transformed into hatred, into a sadistic urge for destruction of the scapegoat. Man destroys what he does not permit himself to love or to be loved by. One of my patients, a white man with strong feelings against racial integration, had transformed his early deep attachment to his colored wet nurse and "mammy" into a racial hatred covering up his deep incestuous yearnings for her.

These antagonistic feelings are further complicated and distorted by the magic fear of mutilation and castration. The circumcized Jew is unconsciously identified with the punishing authority who threatens those who surpass sexual rules with a token castration. Thus we can recognize some aspects of racial hatred as a conversion and outlet of unbalanced sexual and instinctual development. We hate what we fight and struggle against in ourselves.

Collective hatred and the confusing pressure by a minority

How confusing the ideal-sounding principles of nationality and freedom can be has been demonstrated on the Island of Cyprus. Here for several years an unhappy struggle had been going on against so-called British colonialism. However, before the battle for freedom and for return to Greece started, most of the people—as yet untouched by political slogans—felt rather happy under British "oppression" and did not suffer under the auto-suggestion of persecution and oppression. What is more confusing is that Cyprus has, besides the eighty per cent Greek people, a minority population of twenty per cent Turkish people —on an island only thirty miles from Turkey's southern coast but a distance of five hundred miles from Greece. The moment the colonial "oppressor" intended to leave the island, an internal war threatened to begin—not because of realities, freedom, happiness, emotional needs, but because of certain *semantic catch-words* and principles of prestige implanted in the people for obscure political purposes. During the three-year period before the turmoil began, no Cypriot emigrated to Greece; 2600 emigrated to England; 720 to other parts of the British Commonwealth; and 70 to the United States. These figures tell us something about the Cypriots' hidden preferences; but these were preferences the individual could not openly express on the island because of inner political terror exerted by a fanatic, terrorizing minority which informed the majority that one *had* to feel anti-British and, therefore, persecuted.

Temporarily the prejudice of a terrorizing minority can have a tremendous impact. The newcomer takes over its suggestions readily, giving up his initial "bias of objectivity." His deeper wish to be accepted by the group lets him surrender his reasonableness. People are prisoners of their environments, especially of those minorities that mentally coerce their environment.

Pathological personalities like Hitler can acquire all the aspects of such a terrorizing minority. People look at them with blind spots, not seeing their pathology and their prejudices out of fear that by seeing and acknowledging those abnormalities, private inner tensions may be triggered off. Out of neurotic defenses and irrational expectation they submit their rational judgment to the terrorizing minority and the psychopathic tyrant.

All this explains why universal suffrage as such is no solution. It may mean an appeal to universal prejudice under the impact of terrorizing suggestions of a minority! It is often the simple appeal to the traditional frustrations in people that acts more strongly than the appeal to reason.

Vox populi often means the voice of collective frustration, though at other times, without the impact of terror and fear, it can be an appeal to the potential intellect of the people.

Low-brow hates high-brow

But there is also the opposite process: primitive man envies and at the same time hates cultured man. Paradoxically he may provoke his own persecution. Basically his indignation and hostility are inspired by the fear of losing face, the fear of feeling inferior, the fear of being absorbed into something bigger and more differentiated. The retreat to prejudice often results from inability to comprehend actual problems.

In the individual prejudices and hostilities, however, there may also be noted a temporary symptom of growth, of a phase in the maturation process of the personality. Especially in puberty do we witness these conflicts, as the adolescent struggles to become a free independent ego. The burgeoning hatreds result from the subtle inner struggle between the need for self-distinction and the need to identify with others. Parents are mostly much more the victim of this process of individuation than racial minorities. But it explains why those rebellious youths are so easy to exploit for such policies of persecution.

National collectivities also are subject to periods of conflict during maturation. Much self-hatred and resentment toward others stems from the disappointing sudden awareness of man's own limits and desires. The battle between Utopia and reality is continually going on in man. In every hatred people take revenge for this inner frustration. It is so much easier to blame and hate somebody else than to confess limited capacity and self-hatred. Nevertheless, in every hatred lies embodied a deeper realization of incapacity, of impotence—hence, the association of hatred with suicidal fantasies. What we hate is something inside ourselves. We hate our limitations; and that self-hatred usually gets projected onto somebody else, the persecuted scapegoat, the eternal enemy from without.

All the irrational elements of hatred are spread over the entire personality, from mere upheaval of the lowest instinctive functions to the biting justifications produced by the highest intellectual faculties When those irrational elements find overt expression, they are indicative of inner disharmony and disintegration. Yet it takes energy to succeed in breaking through the control of clever ego-defenses.

The opportunity to hate, however, given officially to the individual by a rebellious collectivity or a pathological leader, can set the repressed and frustrated drives free more easily. Now the people can use national catchwords, racial discrimination and collective fury to justify their private hatreds. *Collective hatred, therefore, consists of heterogeneous elements.*

We find even more violent hate-reactions if the control of man's piloting ego has been eliminated, as in cases of mental illness or intoxication. In such cases the instincts have been disconnected from any central guidance. In psychotic cases we can observe hatred in its most genuine and undisguised forms—experienced, for example, in cases of pathological murder.

In psychiatric practice it often remains difficult to uncover instinctive hatred, because it is often so deeply repressed or because the individual disguises it with theoretical justifications. The collectivity, particularly, is the more eager to accept secondary motivations and rationalizations about the enemy from without in order to transform them into national slogans. In collective hatred, in chauvinism and racial discrimination, nearly everyone finds opportunity to air and ventilate some personal aggressive impulses. We may speak here of man's unlimited capacity for transmutation and distortion of his private hatreds. The individual, after having responded to collective suggestions and being fanaticized by the aggressive ecstasy, has less inner mental work to do to motivate his hostile feelings. He uses the externalized hatred in order to give free rein to his (disguised) inner hatred. *Collective hatred saves the individual emotional energy*. That is why it is so much easier to preach hatred and abuse than to lead the world by love.

The role of the group-psyche and group cohesion

As has been mentioned before, some unconscious roots of hatred in the individual's life are connected with frustrated sexuality. Even in the smallest group, the marriage relation, the hidden and ambivalent attitude toward the sexual partner may increase by too much rivalry and mutual comparison. As soon as lovers begin to measure each other's qualities, as a remnant of infantile rivalry and competition, mutual desire and attractiveness will decrease and may turn into envy and jealousy, and finally into hatred and aggression.

With regard to mass psychology, however, these competitive feelings have to be considered from a different point of view. Mass-emotions usually act on a different mental level: they are more contagious, nearer to the immediate impulse and drive, they are more mobile, less motivated, and connected more immediately with the need for participation, group formation and togetherness. Hatred against *another* group—the out-group—is often accompanied by greater inter-individual esteem and love of members of the in-group. The so-called hate-less individual, who can check his private resentments rather well, may still hate as a participating member of his collectivity. Some of the members of the S.S. I had to investigate were apparently different men inside the concentration camp and outside it. Inside they were the most brutish fellows toward the Jews, outside the gentlest fathers and friends.

The aim of a group, be it national, racial, or political, does not necessarily entail hatred against specific other groups. Yet the unobtrusive aim to prevent inner tension in the group may easily be displaced and acted out toward outside groups. Rivalry and hatred are, however, sometimes greatest between politically almost identical formations. This sounds paradoxical. But those who are acquainted with the tremendous storms of early sibling rivalry also understand why political election periods provoke the most bitter hostilities.

The quality of the binding cohesive forces and motivations within the group, above all, determines the feelings toward other groups. Unknown biological elements may play a part here, inasmuch as they are connected with special physical and psychological needs of the group. Groups with weak internal ties, and lots of internal turmoil—built perhaps on a one-sided purpose or on an unstable motivation, e.g., political indignation and enforced ideology or even nihilism—easily foster hatred against competing formations. Sleeping social resentment is a great breeder of racial discrimination. The defeat of the South still is an important factor in their racialistic attitude.

Cohesive ties are a vital condition for the existence of the group. There exist touching stories of spontaneous group formation in concentration camps where people of different religion, different race, different political belief found each other in a common struggle against the cruel jailer and oppressor. They swore each other eternal friendship and loyalty. But immediately after the liberation, they went back to their old separation.

Every criticism or weakening of the vital cohesive ties may shake the group and the security of its individual members. It cannot tolerate internal threat or competition. By its externally directed hatred and prejudice it fights for its own inner existence. The less inner strength and security a group possesses, the more aggressive it will be. *Collective hatred is coupled with internal weakness. It is motivated by the hidden fear about the group's emotional stability, inner cohesion and collective existence.*

Now let us go back for a while to the problem of anti-Semitism and racial prejudice. The Jews constitute a centuries-old social and religious group, one of the oldest known in present-day civilization, with extremely strong inner ties as a reaction formation to outside persecution. The secondary qualities connected with this cohesive strength, as love of the family, charitable care for the co-religionist, the faculty always to recognize each other and the readiness mutually to protect each other, are more conspicuous in the Jews than in other people. Strangely enough, religion was not so much the binding factor; it had become hardened into rigid dogmas and compulsive rituals which, in general, are only professed by small minorities in their midst. Only a minority was orthodox and regular churchgoers. Nor was race the determining factor. One cannot even speak of the Jews as a biological racial unit, for the admixture of other races (Mongols, Moors, Slavs) is clearly discernible.

Historically, it is known that the Jews in East Europe and the Caucasus especially made many converts among surrounding people. It is rather the customs and taboos of an old distinctive culture, and the experience of persecution suffered together, that constitute the most important elements of their group cohesion.

Both the latter elements are extremely important in the creation of a powerful aggregate.

Common reminiscences produce strong ties of friendship. Cultured man is a peculiarly melancholy being, always intent on collecting records: happy memories or tragic reminiscences. (Snapshots and "Kodakmania" are a symptom of this compulsive inner build-up of mementos.) The lives of the Jewish heroes in the Book of Books have become the guiding lights for others.

The mutual charity and solicitude of the Jews is proverbial. Members of a minority who suffer the same fate are forced to like each other. However, people love one another to a lesser extent than might be expected from their fate-conditioned group connection. It is this withered, limited love of man that many novelists have chosen for their subject. Jacob Wasserman speaks of the "inertia of love," of love that is conditional and full of reservations. Jewish cosmopolitan feeling, based on enforced membership of a persecuted, international minority, also became an additional cause of Jew-hatred for a chauvinistic-minded persecutor. This vicious circle has never been broken. In times when nationalism flares up, every stranger and foreigner becomes a scapegoat, and discrimination will be stirred up automatically. Every community in such an aggressive state cunningly searches for the most vulnerable scapegoat, in order not to hurt its own public conscience too much.

To explain German anti-Semitism some students pointed out the specific differences between Jews and Germans which they believed to be connected with differences in biological, instinctive foundation of the personality. Although one cannot speak of *the Jew* and *the German* as anthropological racial units, some of the respective customs of the two groups were of a different quality and must be explained from a difference in reactive behavior patterns. There were, for instance, the different preferences for certain kinds of food; there were very marked differences in emotionality and mental tempo, and also a difference in more differentiated subtle expression of their psychological structure. The German in his peaceful phase is a romanticist and a "Gemuetsmensch," the Jew more of a mystic-rationalist. To the former, the tradition of preparing himself for a heroic death—especially accentuated by the Nazi ideology—appeared as a religious ideal; the latter professed belief in the wealth and happiness of actual life on earth. *The persecuted always build a monument of liberty and happiness into their philosophy.*

It seems to me, however, that these antagonisms cannot be reduced to racial differences. Although "characterology" as the theory of various human reaction patterns is still in its very beginnings, we do know at least that we meet with such variation in reaction pattern in all social communities. *The differences in character inside the group are greater than the apparent differences in general behavior between groups and races.*

Similarly, representatives of the Negro race may seemingly present overall differences in behavior pattern: one may meet with greater impulsiveness and, no matter how cultured the individual Negro may be, with an easier regression and access to primitive reactions than in other races. This is evidenced, for example, in their love of bright colors and primitive music. However, even these apparent differences can be easily explained by a conditioned reaction as a result of the age-long exclusion from cultural traditions and a reaction-formation to persecution and enslavement It is not an essential difference.

Unfortunately, socio-psychological studies about the overall characterological structure of the various races are hardly existent as yet. Here is a large field almost unexplored by scientific research.

It is important to note that frequently there is little or no aversion toward the *individual* Negro in individuals of other races. It is always the image of the group of different *people* that appeals to man's mythical feelings about them. Children have no notion at all of racial difference or inferiority. It has to be taught to them. It is the group that accepts and feels aversion and objects to mixing with the other group. The group as such apparently does not tolerate differences so easily on a biological or cultural level. This is especially fortified by unconscious fantasies about marrying somebody from the out-group or from a different race. Mixed marriage is unconsciously looked upon as an incestuous marriage. As said before, the ominous question in the South, "Would you like your daughter to marry a Negro?", is a displacement of repressed incestuous wishes. The unconscious translates it: "I don't like the Negro to do what I would like to do, but don't dare to confess to myself."

Through mixing of different groups, formative ties of the in-group threaten to be broken and the continuity of each group itself seems endangered. In the Congo one can actually see what emotions are aroused when the existence of the tribal society is threatened. Sometimes during such upheaval there is envy implied of the vitally stronger group. There even exists envy of the persecuted ones because they have real reason to regress and to feel depressed.

In actuality, however, individuals of different races *irresistibly attract each other.* Nature seems to demand compensation and crossbreeding. The noted German psychiatrist and investigator of individual and racial differences, Kretschmer, has pointed out that such mixtures are biologically justified—especially so if previously there had been strong inbreeding in the group resulting in weakening and degenerative symptoms. Groups also die! In order to survive and to become more vital, groups also need merging and copulation, just as individuals do. Racial mixture and more intensive mutual association lead to a better genetic adjustment to environment, promoting the formation of better adapted new species.

Old races, old communities with inbreeding attract each other; but there is vacillation and ambivalence in the very attraction brought about, as it were, at the expense of the old, stable order. They want to live in isolation and they want to merge. Love and mutual hatred will fluctuate until a new balance of relations is established.

The variation in group cohesion

In the antagonism between groups and social formations, differences in inner group cohesion and group tradition often are of greater importance than biological racial differences. This is partly rooted in the various motivations for joining a group. People can join the same group out of contrasting motives, but the group instinctively protects itself against those who threaten to spoil the club.

The inter-human ties grow more refined, however, with age and persistency of culture. Culture is the continuously transmitted spiritual possession of the group. The social group derives its most important strength from such cultural ties. Strong, matured cultural ties prevail over those of younger groups. What is culturally inferior, physically powerful though it may be, is frequently absorbed into what is culturally higher. The group, unlike the individual, does not subserve the satisfaction of biological impulses. It wants more; it wants to create safeguards for instinctual life and, in doing so, to provide the opportunity for higher cultural development. *The significance of every group formation is the creation of internal psychic stability and a field for cultural evolution.*

Within the various groups we always observe a struggle on two fronts The culturally younger and the culturally older regard each other as hostile The group as such aims at self-preservation; mixing with groups on a different level of development always means the breaking of old ties, the giving up of habits and beliefs, and becoming more tolerant about rigid rules and rites, but it may also mean losing the inner backbone which culture and tradition provide.

Three factors determine the nature and stability of the group: 1) the force of inner coherence—*formative strength;* 2) its cultural evolution—*stage of evolution;* and 3) sense and motive of being together—*formative purpose.* The undermining of any of these factors will be regarded by the group as a hostile act.

The political opposition is always hated for having an antagonistic aim. But this hatred can be a *sporting, tolerant* hatred, an activating element—as we find it, for instance, between Labor and Tories in England. Yet, unconsciously, the minority party is identified with those who break down the stability of the nation.

However, the competing group, with parallel aims, is often felt as much more dangerous, for it threatens to break the inner strength of one's own group. A *bitter* hatred may arise between such political groups, coupled with ambition, fury and mutual reproach as is, for instance, the case between Democratic Socialists and totalitarian Communists. Although their goals were originally the same or nearly so, bitter hatred developed about the methods of achieving these goals. Communism, because of its ruthless overemphasizing of certain means to reach an economic goal, grew into a monolithic totalitarianism.

But a totally different developmental trend and a different cultural rhythm of another group are also felt as hostile. The mass reaction to this may be a confused hatred. Respect and bitterness, attraction and repulsion, the capacity and the wish to understand, admiration and abuse—all go into the building of this complicated effect, as can be witnessed in the competitive relations between American big business and the Russian totalitarian system. The fusion of different races also arouses these feelings of confusion, because both groups feel threatened in their inner cohesion.

Even in group formation among scientists the same may be seen. The young group fighting for its inner stability meets with compulsory conformity and uniformity brought about by fear of internal tensions. Every man with a new theory that threatens to create schism becomes the ever-present enemy and scapegoat and pushes the original group into becoming more orthodox. The actual schisms in psychoanalytic theory are an example of this internal trouble and scientific infancy.

Every stranger who is not understood arouses aversion and suspicion, and this is most apparent when the stranger is a foreigner. One social formation will feel roused and stimulated by the strange "enclave," another will see in it a reflection of its own feelings of inferiority. Disparity in cultural level is, however, more irritating than is generally conceded. Close to the adulation of the more cultured there exists in all groups a tremendous hostility toward creative intelligence, which yet serves as the stabilizer of cultural level. Such intelligence provokes irritation because it is in conflict with a more general human wish for passivity, sleep and apathy.

Many psychological differences between Germans and Jews could be explained by disparity in formative and cultural age and even in developmental level. This was reflected in the type of Nazi hatred it was a "confused" hatred, rationalized in various ways, but no Nazi whom we interrogated during the war was ever able to offer a valid and reasonable explanation. The same was true for the insane mass-killing of Jews. Hitler's hangmen had to delve deep into history to produce even sham justificatory arguments. As a matter of fact, there were more suicides among the guards of the concentration camps than among the inmates.

Genetically seen, the German trend toward myth, romanticism, and "Gemuetlichkeit," as opposed to the predominantly mystic rationality of the Jew, means a difference in personality growth and development. Yet every individual, as detached from the group, has both elements within himself. Romanticism is usually a phase of puberty full of "Weltschmerz," world-pain, preceding the adult experience of achieving integration and unity of personality. Only in, or through, the dominant group persuasions does either of these differences remain. The Jews, as a persecuted group, felt more cosmopolitan, especially after the experiences of age-long dispersal. Through the ages they had promoted the idea of human brotherhood. Their religious ideas bear witness to this all-embracing concept. The Nazi under Hitler looked upon his national group as a more secluded "chosen" formation. To him, nationalism and isolationism sounded identical. Narrow nationalism is hostile to cosmopolitanism, as hatred is hostile to love. Nationalism still believes in the magic of power and conquest. The persecuted Jews, having had to bear the yoke of oppression for ages, have developed a specific sense of justice. The Jewish God, threatening at times, is nevertheless the God of justice, legality and morality, a typical deity for persecuted minorities.

Germans and Jews have had a different line of cultural development; thus their life rhythms must have been different. Neither is better nor worse than the other, but the larger group, having become chauvinistic and aggressive (especially under the hypnotic whip of Nazism), could not tolerate the smaller one, the less so since the latter held up the mirror of a moral and legal path that is extremely difficult to tread for a group in aggressive expansion. Between the Jewish cosmopolitan concept of justice and the German chauvinistic concept of power arose the "persecution mania of the persecutor," of the madman Hitler who imprinted his own delusions on all those who were receptive to them. The brute and the sadist project their own guilt-feelings onto the outside world and, consequently, feel even more persecuted. Hence the brute-sadist will—in anticipation, as it were—become himself increasingly prone to persecution and murder.

And thus Hitler could use the already existing latent German anti-Semitism as a psychological tool to teach many Germans how to become greater brutes and better murderers. That was his way of making a temporary savage gang of criminals out of his people. The in-group always feels itself fortified by the delusion of a common enemy. From that point on they are "in it" together.

The self-defensive motivation and self-justification that prompt all aversion, hatred and discrimination are problems that will remain for a long time in our world. Whenever man's existence, in the narrower sense of the word, is threatened, hostilities of various kinds flare up. We saw that even in England, where we thought that racialism had died out. The search for the eternal enemy from without begins to obscure the inner enemy and inferiority. "They are evil and must be destroyed" is nearly always a projection of the hidden inner evil. Every allegedly "inferior" trait in the other fellow is construed as a justification of one's own hatred and aggression. Actually, all hatred projects man's own uncertainty and weakness onto the imaginary enemy. Above all, in insoluble conflicts, hostility chooses a defenseless scapegoat as an outlet. A small triumph by means of displaced aggression is sought to mask the big inner emptiness and defeat. Therefore, a weak minority has to be accused of all the hideous intents that unconsciously smoulder in the aggressor's own psyche.

Discrimination as a tool of aggression

Our investigation has shown that discrimination and collective hatred as a compound of various factors can be used as an easy means of political agitation, acting just as contagiously as gossip and slander. The agitator looks for a scapegoat to sharpen his attack and to make the inner cohesion of the group tighter. He likes to manipulate these inflaming images (which may be true or untrue). With prejudice and bias one enhances fanatical feelings of greatness in the masses. In and through their daily habits, people no longer realize that they unwittingly have given their mutual daily antipathy and anger a slant in the direction prescribed by official propaganda. Jew-baiting was a pathological symptom not limited to Nazi Germany only. Satanization of the scapegoat takes place everywhere in the world. Racial discrimination, class discrimination, even township discrimination—these occur everywhere in the world. I know people from Manhattan who forever look down on Brooklynites.

An amazingly large number of human beings convert their personal hatred into a general prejudice. Once a person has become entangled or even engulfed in this form of socially accepted resentment, he will interpret all sorts of other phenomena in terms of anti-Semitism, or racialism, and so on. Every depreciation of the scapegoat increases such a man's self-esteem. Gradually a complete persecution mania may develop, such as we saw in the Nazi scheme. The Jew was presented as holding financial power, as the usurer, the perpetual black marketeer. No amount of objective economic and financial statistics was able to disprove this argument; the delusion could not be corrected. Psychologically it is of interest that the right and logically intellectual counter-argument only fortified the delusion and made the hatred more magical. In addition, all sorts of other archaic magic fears cropped up: the Jews used children's blood for their sacrifices, they violated "mother Germany" by raping young Aryan girls. Illustrative examples of such pathological delusions were provided everywhere in Germany by the "*Stuermer*," the sensational newspaper, full of pornography and officially recommended for reading in schools. Horror stories and atrocities exercised a special attraction and played on people's fantasy.

However, the propaganda of persecution and imprecation has a still deeper magic significance. It allays people's fears. The preoccupation with the scapegoat gives a lift. The cynical technicians of emotional upheaval, guided by their own delusions, are, of course, unaware of those internal contrasts and ambivalences in their own motives. As long as one is persecuting scapegoats—the Jews, or the Negroes, or the Yellow Race, or the Wall Street Capitalists—one feels inwardly sure that danger will pass one's own door Even if one pities the victims, that secret magic protective thought continues to have its safeguarding effect. "Better that they be sacrificed than that we be persecuted." Scapegoatism is always escape from inner battle!

It is curious to notice that the worst anti-Semites and racists know least about the Jews as such, or about races in general. They usually have good relations with a few private Jews, whom they show off as their friends, and whom they call exceptions to their rules, but "the Jews" in general are an object of complete magic horror to them.

Thus anti-Semitism and racial hatred stem from a magic horror and mythical depth usually more often appearing in uncultured people. "Jew-mania" is for the primitive, paranoiac personality a nightmare besieging his would-be greatness. In the last resort, it is a fear of the imaginary Jew himself, that is, of an uncanny uninhibited or unmanageable animal within that he can no longer control The word "Jew" is an obsession for the anti-Semite, a magical complex of diabolical fears It represents something he fears in himself that he doesn't want to face.

People frequently will battle with those destructive inner fantasies, using various justifying arguments which, in turn, they will discard again and again. People enjoy talking about scapegoats and their "objectionable" qualities in order to relieve their tensions. The art of gossiping is based on this temporary relief of one's tensions through vituperation of those who are absent.

One cannot fight anti-Semitism and racial discrimination by mere emotional or even intellectual arguments, since it has nothing to do with the actual, verbalized conflicts. The presence of a discriminating attitude only indicates the presence of pressing unconscious conflicts in the haters which seek an easy outlet. Therefore the extent of anti-Semitism and racialism or scapegoatism is a valuable gauge of inner tensions and cultural level of a people. In the colonial age, for instance, the original need for economic exploitation of a more primitive race acquired greater justification through psychological discrimination. The superiority complex was used as a shield, as a defense against the inner guilt of economic abuse.

Fear and discrimination

The present flowering forms of discrimination and racial hatred and so many other manifestations of mass-hatred prove how severely man's existence is threatened in all its foundations, both economic and spiritual. Neither the individual nor the collectivity feels secure any longer. Culture wavers. Without realizing the deeper meaning of these projections, the more powerful collectivities create scapegoat-clichés; the pacifist, the wandering Jew, the Colonialist, the Communist, the Negro, the Capitalist and the like. Hostile nationalism is on the upsurge. In most countries these disintegrative tendencies meet with a wide response. Personal freedom is at bay. The powerful group wants to rule and the individual is denied the right to profess allegiance to the group or philosophy of his choice.

Is present-day culture in some particular way responsible for the emergence of these tendencies toward mass-hatred? Can we attribute such reaction to, for example, an arrested (rigid) state of cultural development which is being pierced by a dynamic anti-intellectual and anti-democratic thrust? Is this the age of unreason? Only the future can answer this question. Actually many of the motivations offered for collective hatred and race supremacy are associated with anti-intellectual currents. In the

Nazis a vague feeling of hatred against an over-intellectual culture had become linked with an old collective hatred against a people that imagined itself to be the Chosen One. This attitude used to arouse jealousy and envy, above all in the economic and cultural fields. It is the Germans' double tragedy that they, under Hitler's guidance, transplanted the old religious delusive ideas of the Jews of being "God's own people" to their own "Master Race." The cult of the Master Race temporarily served to counteract their collective feeling of inferiority after a lost war. Mankind is now going through a general feeling of inferiority because of feelings of estrangement in a cold, technical, push-button world. This attitude of resentment does not, however, preserve culture and social ties; not even man's material need is satisfied in this way. Inner despair grows, and thus the group may move toward a crisis which only ushers in a new wave of rebelliousness against culture and civilization.

The contagious aspects of discrimination

Because the need for scapegoats—the need to externalize inner tensions—is universal, it can be easily aroused in other people unless one has learned to face this inner mental defense mechanism. Gossip, slander, malingering—these always find a willing ear in the search for the eternal enemy. Unwittingly many people will willy-nilly be dragged into the stream of somebody else's vituperations, simply because this releases some inner tension

Mostly our surrender to mental contagion starts with small inner self-betrayal when, for instance, we don't protest against somebody's gossip, even when we are aware that it is untrue. The need to be an accepted member of an intimate and cozy gossiping group is usually greater than to be the one who courageously defends the slandered outsider. This subtle giving in to group suggestion is at the core of every propagandistic success. All psychological warfare, therefore, uses the weapon of unreasonable slander and vituperation to arouse the emotions needed to make a willing, submissive group out of a crowd.

"Look at the bastard, the scapegoat!" By giving people the opportunity to externalize and displace the hatred from within, the mental contagion spreads.

Because prejudice contains such a strong contagious and traditional element, we may say it is nearly man's second nature. It can be aroused in anybody under the heavy impact of propaganda and mass-contagion. It represents the deep fear of getting away from the vertical traditional tribal and family relations and also from the horizontal social participations.

It represents the deep fear of being a lonely individual!

Discrimination and racialism degenerate easily into a contagious disease because they reverberate in everybody's personal complexes. That is the reason why a minority can terrorize a majority into the delusion of discrimination. Because nearly everybody is afraid to be excommunicated if he protests!

The fearless don't hate

Every analysis of feelings of mass-hatred and discrimination points to the paramount necessity of deflecting man's fear and hostility into politically productive channels. Collectivities should, however, learn to detect and understand the fearful anticipations that are continually being aroused in them. One of the new aims should be to learn to tolerate inner tensions in the service of greater tolerance and a multiple approach to truth.

Every kind of hatred has an inner source. The search for the elusive enemy in us serves to release intolerable tension in group and community. Hater and hated alike take part in that collective feeling. If you dislike yourself, you are much better off hating somebody else! That is why antipathy and vengeance are so much more in favor than tolerance and justice. All our movies and comic books are full of the ever-present enemy and scapegoat that gets punished.

Can we convince and convert prejudiced people? It will be difficult indeed for the mass to realize their prejudice and to foster this realization, because it is so easy now to make them feel they themselves are scapegoats and are persecuted.

It is dangerous now to let the American South feel itself the victim of public opinion, because this only hardens the South's feelings. Moral pressure is needed which is stronger than the terror inside. An emotional conversion hardly ever occurs through insight; some deep inner crisis is needed. All the more important, therefore, that those who influence the masses through whatever means of communication (press, radio, television, books, film, and so on) understand this point. Assimilation of new moral habits is a slow process.

It is dangerous indeed to exploit the effects of latent fear and mass-hatred Outbursts of mass emotions are nearly always senseless: inevitably the aroused hatred turns against people themselves in the end. This means that the group that breeds hatred will gradually commit suicide, its social structure will disintegrate. Hatred and persecution always have weakened persecutors and persecuted alike.

Those who imagine themselves lost hate each other. They live in mortal fear of death and destruction. Great men and great nations do not hate and despise because they realize that for creating a culture, there must be a persistent social formation, however imperfect its workings may be.

CHAPTER FOUR

The New Technical Age

When I get up in the morning, I turn on my radio to hear the news and the weather forecast. But then come the coercive voices telling me to take aspirin for my headache. I have a "headache" occasionally (as does the rest of the world), and my headaches, like everyone else's, come from the many conflicts and challenges that life imposes on me. But my radio tells me not to think about either the conflicts or the unpleasant headaches. It suggests, instead, that I retreat into an ancient magic action—swallowing medicine. Although I laugh as I listen to this long-distance prescription by persuasive salesmen far removed from me and my headache, and even meditate for a moment on man's servility to the magic of chemistry, my hand has already—automatically—begun to reach out for the aspirin bottle. After all, I do have a headache!

It is difficult, indeed, to escape the mechanically repeated slogans of everyday life. In the world of advertisers there is no greater Utopia outside the increased consumption of appliances.

Even when our critical senses reject the suggestions, they slip beneath the barrier of our critical comprehension and seduce us into doing what our intellect tells us is stupid. The new age with its amazing inventions has confronted man with enormous challenges, demanding of him a new awareness of what is going on in his inner and outer world. The core of the question is, will man be able to control the tremendous forces he has unleashed?

The technicalization and mechanization of modern life have already influenced people to become more passive and to adjust themselves to ready-made conformity. The confidence in the machine replaces man's belief in his own vitality and initiative. The headlines in the morning paper give man his temporary political outlook; the radio blasts suggestions into his ears; television keeps him in continual awe and passive fixation. Consciously man may protest against all these anonymous voices, but nevertheless, their suggestions ooze into his system.

What is most shocking about these technological influences is that many of them have developed not out of man's destructiveness but out of his urge to discover and improve his world and to make life richer and deeper. The very institutions man has created to help himself, the very tools he has made towards mastery of himself and his environment—all these can become weapons of self-destruction and downfall.

The growth of technology, for example, the development of the thousands of mechanical gadgets designed to serve both our social needs and our individual fantasies, can easily have a debilitating effect on man's maturity and mental integrity, throwing him back into an infantile dream of unlimited omnipotence. There he sits, the bored human animal, all alone in his room with all kinds of magic knobs around him. But let him just push a button, and as by a miracle he can change his world. What power! And what even greater might the little magician envisions! Yet what danger is inherent in such an idea!

The growth of technology, instead of helping man, may weaken him in his struggle for mental maturity. Technique, the making of tools, was originally intended to give man more security against outside physical forces. It safeguarded his world, and it freed his time and energy for meditation, concentration and creation. However, the man-made tools themselves have gradually taken possession of man, and have unwittingly pushed him back to a peculiar serfdom instead of towards liberation. Man is no longer master of his tools. Technology, in its acme—symbolized by a stockpile of H-bombs—has become the most frightening monster of our era.

Paradoxically enough, technical security and the dangerous myth of technical progress may take away challenge and increase man's cowardice. The mechanical spoon-fed world we ourselves have created has replaced the very vital challenge which nature originally afforded man's imagination, and man is no longer compelled to face alone the forces of nature outside himself and the forces of instinct within him. Mechanized life has scheduled all these forces; our social habits and rituals think, as it were, for us. Our luxurious habits and complicated civilization have a tendency to appeal more to our mental passivity, conformism and submission than to our spiritual alertness and moral commitment. The daily barrage of advertising pipes feelings of unwitting dissatisfaction into our minds. Mentally passive people, without basic morals and philosophy, are easily lured into political adventures that are in conflict with the ethics of a free democratic society.

The new age of technical leisure has become perilous indeed, because for many people leisure has become an empty time-space. True, there exists active creative leisure, but there is also passive leisure, a surrender and regression to mere animal drives. There exists active play and passive diversion, mental play and surrender to sleepwalking.

Technique and technology may encourage man to think of himself as gigantic and omnipotent, but on the other hand they make him feel weak, tiny and inferior—a cog in a wheel, or a wheel among wheels. The assembly line alienates man from his work, from the concept of his own constructive labor. No longer does man produce directly the things he needs; the machine produces for him. Engineers and scientists tell us that in the near future automation—running factories with a minimum of human help—will become a reality, and human labor and human inventiveness will become almost superfluous.

How can man have self-esteem and self-reliance if he becomes the most expendable part of his world? The ethical and moral values that are the foundation of our free democratic society are based on the view that human life and human happiness are the earth's greatest goods. But in a society in which the machine takes over completely, all our traditional values can be destroyed. In venerating the machine—and the machine-producing machine—we negate ourselves, we inadvertently begin to believe that might makes right, that the individual human being has no intrinsic worth, and that life itself is only part of a greater technical and chemical thought process.

Man's progressive development towards a mechanized, push-button world is best illustrated by his love for fast planes, automobiles and other speedy machines to conquer time. The moment he can retreat to his car seat and direct the world by remote control, man dreams an old childhood dream of tremendous omnipotence. The raving frenzy, the conquest of space, combined with the sense of power and control the steering wheel gives, seizes the imagination and the passion of practically every driver. Thus man's unconscious drive towards speed and destruction—also called his accident proneness—have made the automobile one of the greatest killers in our society.

Man's servility to his machines takes something away from

his individuality. We all are mesmerized by the idea of remote control. The wheels and the push-buttons give us a false sense of outer freedom while we pay no attention to control of inner psychic forces. We dream of the conquest of universal outer space, while inner space—man's psyche—has remained a riddle to us.

But at the same time, the creative part of man tries to resist the machine's cold mechanical intrusion into his inner freedom. We all dream, somehow, of poetic leisure, of relaxation and of being in tune with the universe.

Every time I pass something beautiful along the road as I drive my car—be it an exhilarating view, a museum, a river, a tall tree —at that very moment a kind of tense ambivalence is aroused in me. Shall I stop the car and drink in the beauty around me, or shall I give in to my motor and keep racing along?

For the psychologist and biologist such behavior raises important questions. How will it end? Will man's tendency to become more and more an immobile technological embryo finally get the better of him and his civilization?

The Dutch anatomist Bolk—one of my teachers—long ago described the retardation in growth characteristic of the human animal as compared to the rapid development of the higher primates. As a result of this so-called fetalization and anatomical retardation of man, man acquired his erect posture, the use of his grasping and verifying hands, the possibility of speech and learning, a long youth and dependence on the paternal nest. This long youth made it possible for him to play more, to learn more, and to build up his own thought world.

However, since the Renaissance many a scientist has retreated more and more to his technological womb, his laboratory, his study, his armchair. From his magic corner of scholarship he proposes (in his imagination) to control the world with his inventions and mental dictates. The inherent danger in such specialization and fragmentation of knowledge and research is the unwitting departure from a broad, moral, humanistic basis of thinking about and "verifying" the world. The loss of coherence and integration of knowledge inadvertently regresses part of the investigating personality and unwittingly provokes hostile debunking drives in him toward competitive scholars.

In the meantime the idea of cosmic awareness and religious fathoming of the unknown becomes repressed and denied. The compulsion to invent and discover urges him toward specialization and he loses an eye for the overall integration of forces and man's limitation of knowledge.

The mechanized intellect with its strictly causal mechanical approach and its "nothing-but" formula denies vitality, hope and faith and its own mental restrictions. Such scholars are possessed of an obsessive positivism while denying all inner doubt and ambivalence. They have become captives of their personal curiosity without granting the other fellow his curiosity and different approach to problems of the universe. There exists an invention and discovery compulsion based on infantile, magic need to feel the power of gadgets.

"What are we inventing for?" That is the moral question. In its neurotic need, technological science arrogantly fights its own limitations and in its angry mood it grows biased and often denies what it observes. True, there also exists in man a form of creative discovery, creative in humility and ecstatic joy. But the danger of the technical pattern is that one tends to fall into a persuasive closed logic, easily leading to captivity within one's own system and probable destruction of the systems of others. The result is a dogmatic sticking to one's own theory in the service of some magical remote control of other people.

More and more the population has been seduced by the idea of remote control without being ripe for exercising such power. The arsenal of buttons and gadgets leads people unwittingly into the infantile dream of omnipotent power. Our technical civilization gives us greater ease, yet it is challenge and uneasiness that makes for character and strength. The shortest way is not the best way. The increase of leisure and ease take the challenge away from life. We live in an age in which ease and idleness are characteristic, and we have not yet learned to understand their deteriorating influences. Healthy, strong egos are not formed by luxury and leisure. Every form of self-preservation and self-assertion implies the acceptance of pain and suffering in the service of more worthy goals. Our whole system of fair sports training is based on that fact. Many little pains thicken the skin. Yet our aspirin age indulges in the avoidance of small pains and denial of the great ones.

The dangerous paradox in the boost of living standards, for instance, is that it promotes ease, idleness and laziness and yearning for greater ease and passivity. The mind falls asleep and becomes an automaton itself. No future goal is imagined anymore. There exists a fear of ideology and Utopia, which are after all the only means to battle the wrong ideologies. Such technical living can make highly specialized primitives out of us who use the machine either to destroy our own boredom or that of others. The tension of the emptiness of boredom is not well understood in our era. When the mind cannot fill the feeling of emptiness and deprivation, war may burst out if only to break the tension of boredom and misused leisure. Mankind has to get away from the seductive call for leisure and laziness telling us that lack of challenge is the best life.

Just as we are gradually replacing human labor by machines, so we are gradually replacing the human brain by mechanical computers, and thus are unwittingly increasing man's sense of unworthiness. We begin to picture the mind itself as a computing device, as a mere sum total of electrochemical impulses and actions.

The brain as an organ of the mind is also an organ of the body; its structure and its actions can be studied and examined. But the mind itself is a very different concept. It is not alone the sum total of the physiological processes in the brain, it is more than that: it is also the unique, steering and creative aspect of the human personality. The mind pictured as a machine implies denial of or, at the very least, the minimization of emotional life and the value of inner experience. In such a leveled-off picture of man, spontaneity and creativity will never be understood though man may know everything about the tools of the mind.

Unless we watch ourselves, unless we become more aware of the serious problems our technology has brought us, our entire society could turn into a kind of super-technological state in which man becomes a conforming, servile tool of an inhuman "system" instead of a unique free individual.

Man, whose welfare should be the goal of society, would thus become merely a means by which to achieve the goal of efficiency for the system. This system of technocracy—based on the morality of computers—could easily bring about organized brutality and the crushing of any personal feeling of morality. In such a mechanically-minded society any set of values can be forcibly imprinted on the unconscious mind. This, after all, is how Pavlov conditioned his dogs. Any breakdown of moral awareness and of the individual's sense of his own worth makes us more vulnerable to mental coercion.

All this may sound extreme. But the fact is that any influence —overt or concealed, well- or ill-intentioned—which reduces man's alertness and his capacity to face reality as an investigative human being, which reduces the sense of responsibility as active individual, takes from people some part of their essential humanness. Any influence, technical or political, which tends to rob man of his free verifying mind can reduce him to robotism Any influence which destroys man's individuality can destroy the whole society.

The half-truths concerning our world that we read in headlines and news digests may weaken our strength and reinforce our infantile need for greater security. In our world we have to earn real insight through daily mental struggle. Knowledge and insight have to be won, achieved day by day.

Such is our actual picture of modern civilization—so thin a veneer over primitive man that it scarcely disguises him, with so chaotic and uncertain a future that he is easily driven into periodic rebellious savagery. People no longer know how to deal with their liberties or their luxuries.

Can we cope with our civilization? Will a new desire for stability and awareness of our own difficulties succeed in resolving these many contradictions? Is man able to meet the moral challenges in order to achieve physical and mental freedom, or will he succumb to easy slavery?

The answer to these questions will depend on how man will be able to face and unravel the web of suggestions and coercions that keep his mind caught. The moral questions of life are never technical.

Our civilization, although unstable, has to be defended against invasions from lower civilizations. The rich culture of the Aztecs got lost because of an incompetent defense against the Spanish conquistadores. Roman civilization disintegrated in the war against the Barbarians mainly because of inner weakness and decadence.

What will happen to Western civilization? Will it survive? Can it be stabilized, differentiated, perfected? The only thing we can say now is that it has a better chance than any other civilization has had in the past—if it can use its historical and anthropological knowledge and insight in order *not to repeat the mistakes of the past.* A variety of cultural forms will always exist and co-exist. Variety is necessary for continual growth and rejuvenation. Homogeneity of cultural forms usually means death.

Cross-fertilization is needed to keep a culture alive. Inbreeding of human habits is just as lethal as sexual inbreeding.

Every growth and development is an evolution from vague lower forms to more precise higher forms. From less differentiated inherent qualities develop more perfectly and consciously directed values. In other words, the hidden potentialities develop in sound, goal-directed behavior. Modern techniques of communication and travel prevent the decline or disappearance of cultural forms and values, and there can be a transposition of cultural forms from one civilization center to another. We live in an age of constant moving and rapid change. Twentieth-century man travels around very easily; in the seventeenth century he moved about with much greater difficulty; yet, many emigrants carried their culture with them and took root in far-off parts of the world. Those who refused to submit to tyranny and persecution bore the banners of their freedom to other parts of the world.

Civilization cannot be regulated from a central point; that is the method of dictatorships. Totalitarian thought-control and fascistic "Kultur Kammers" destroy civilization. An excess of uniformity and regulation disturbs the natural order; rigidity of mind suffocates the spontaneity and creativity of life.

All human beings are the heirs of millions of other human beings who left behind them traces of their civilizations condensed in language and literature. Are we able to embrace these inherited values? Can we inherit and comprehend past knowledge and insight? Is there an evolution of man's brain power parallel to the evolution of man's civilization? We don't know exactly. But modern psychology tends to answer "yes," providing the personal learning and training period lasts long enough. It is a clinical maxim that we have to pay our tribute of neurotic traits and frustrations thanks to the fact that we can better check our instinctual drives.

Man is the animal with the longest youth. Physically and

mentally he remains a dependent child for a very long time, but this offers him the tremendous opportunity of continuous learning and ripening and controlling himself.

Man *must* learn that, because of his specific type of mental development, his power lies primarily in his social, adaptive capacities. Physical and technical power is only a borrowed power. It is our psychological growth and maturation that will decide what we will do with our explosive toys, with our atomic power. At present it would seem, as Freud put it, that "we are living beyond our psychological means."

The principal difference between our modern civilization and past epochs is that we now have a science of the human being upon which to chart possibilities. Anthropology, psychology and sociology can give us the means to chart our own history. New frontiers affording adventurous exploration are gone. Colonialism is dead. The geography of our planet is now sufficiently known. Gone are the buccaneers and the individual adventurers. Rather than an expanding, fighting world with the adventure of expanding frontiers, we must now establish a social and moral world. This loss of opportunities for instinctual adventure is one of our modern psychological problems. We must find more productive forms of instinctual satisfaction than gambling and war. New ways of living have to be discovered in which human courage, endeavor and initiative can be trained.

Man is the only animal able to look into the future And this very gift can become a heavy burden, one of fear and anticipated catastrophe. Sometimes there is no actual danger to fear, but man's anticipated, fearful fantasy throws him into a panic, nevertheless.

In the past, human intelligence was concentrated on the conquest of nature, on its powers of growth and destruction. In the future, human intelligence will have to concentrate more and more on the powers of the mind and on the problem of the development of a healthy community. Mental hygiene will be one of the most prominent of future sciences. While technical physicists want to control outer space and travel to the moon, psychologists emphasize the control of inner space.

The fact that man is able to commit suicide and cut off his own mysterious lifeline has always had a peculiar impact on his thinking. In his overawed need for security and absolute certainty, death often became to him more to be wished for than the uncertainty of life. Man can threaten others with his own downfall. Hara-kiri is a ritual that we find back in all civilizations.

We even find very subtly in the urge for mathematical precision and for compulsive perfection and exactitude a hidden destructive factor denying all spontaneity and inherent uncertainty of life. There exists an inherent antinomy between mathematical strictness and exactitude and the feeling of moral goodness. The first one restricts and limits, the last one promotes a sympathetic expansion into the other fellow.

In our atomic age it is theoretically possible to wipe out all life on earth. A couple of hydrogen bombs with a cobalt coating will envelop the earth in a deadly dust for many years to come, no matter where the bomb falls. That's the way the bomb makes an end to man's megalomaniacal complacency.

CHAPTER FIVE

What Ails Our Civilization?

What ails our civilization? Our world is in crisis; not the world of the white race only, but the world of all races, all peoples. We are actually in the midst of a tremendous global convulsion, a process we cannot fully comprehend because our mental capacities are still warped and clouded by a postwar hangover. Hitler predicted that a defeated Germany would drag the world down to its final downfall. The illusion fits into the myths of the masochistic and sadistic fantasies of the infant: the push-button fantasy of a magic destruction. Hitler's prediction of downfall is the same idea that Spengler sold us after the first defeat of Germany in his "Decline of the West."

Only pessimistic voices seem to echo through the postwar world. They announce with Spengler that Western civilization is on the decline. "The individual economic adventurer, the white Croesus has had his day." . . . "Every civilization comes and goes. The same old historical law is occurring again." The picture of cataclysmic horror at the end of our world is part of a

Judaeo-Christian mythology of history, in which the days of Armageddon come before the final return to paradise.

Similar prophetic voices spoke of humanity's decline and the world's downfall during the Renaissance. It is a lively theme for pessimists.

Is ours a dying civilization? This self-condemnatory question is being asked by a shocked and guilty world as it castigates itself for producing a Hitler, a Buchenwald, world wars, a Stalin, a hydrogen bomb All those historians see as they look at the world a development of evil principles only.

What has happened to the human being? Did he really attempt a form of mass suicide in the last war, a war followed by chaos, hunger, suspicion, and destruction? Is it reasonable to be so pessimistic? Shall we be seduced into defeatism because of the difficult tasks of reconstructing the world? Or should we accept the opposite simple dogma of inevitable progress and a golden future?

Psychology teaches us that good and evil belong together as an inherent polar development of growing and becoming. This, then, remains our most crucial question: Is the human being able to check and control his aggressive and self-destructive tendencies and give leeway to more peaceful behavior? Will man always identify civilization with wealth, honor, status, prestige and influence and the power to fight for these "goods"?

Man developed only slowly from his purely zoological beginnings. He became human and led a heroic life wherein he learned to endure and combat not only the material and physical threats from the outside world, but also the psychological dangers from his tumultuous inner world, and the rigid rules of his early civilization.

Because of man's growing consciousness, he lives in a continually expanding inner universe, so much more important for his destiny than outer space. His civilized heritage is constantly growing; sometimes he can cultivate, enlarge, and purify this mental inheritance. But at other times he lacks the capacity to understand his inner mental processes and the more to understand those of others.

There is a continual interrelation between man and his civilization. When, because of disease, slavery, and exhaustion, it is not possible for man to comprehend his own epoch and take his place as full-fledged member in society, the old primitive man in him may come to the fore again, and regression and degeneration may occur. He regresses; his mental capacities become dormant. Such temporary collective regression occurred, for instance, among the Negroes of Central Africa, who, in past ages, reached a rather high level of culture in the Bantu civilization.

In general there are three groups of forces that control the dynamics of civilizations.

1) long-lasting and repeated social habit formations,

2) aggressive and destructive qualities in the individual and group, and

3) positive creative powers, as expressed in religious adoration, the arts, and the sciences.

Sometimes some of these forces seemingly work in the service of destruction, as in war. Too great a domination by one of these civilizing factors may be dangerous to culture. Even organized religion had its destructive phases and wars of intolerance. Culture can be but a pseudo-culture in times when the outer façade of civilized habits and pretense is looked upon as more important than inner integrity, honesty, and reality.

However, it has become increasingly possible for man to mold history to suit himself, for history has developed gradually into a product of human control and creation.

In ancient times civilizations died because of their isolation (e.g., the Mayan civilization), but today the world has become one big crossroad of cultural exchange and diffusion. Technically, influenced by our means of communication, we already live in a world of enforced co-existence, although there are still too many barriers and deep suspicion of opposing ideas and viewpoints. Even the difference between Eastern and Western psyche is a pseudo-difference. Nobody knows better than the doctor that all men are equal. They come to him with identical pains and problems, with the same sadness and ecstasy. Man falls in love, children are born, a man dies.

When I had my first Chinese patient in psychoanalytic treatment, I expected difficulties. My not-too-precise knowledge of Oriental culture had inspired me with awe and respect for our oldest existing civilization, but it had also given me a feeling of strangeness, of something eerie that my mind could not grasp. My expectations were wrong The treatment proceeded in exactly the same way as with my other patients, despite linguistic difficulties that obliged us to communicate in a language not our own. The old eternal human problems were the same: a childhood with difficult, quarreling parents, a harsh school in a country torn by war, rivalry with an older brother, the loss of a beloved bride. It was the same outpouring of the crying child as I had experienced with other patients. Sometimes there was the special background of Oriental rites, for my patient it was always a pleasure to explain to me this exotic, unfamiliar world. Yet, it was the intense, human contact in our explorative collaboration that helped him to solve his conflicts.

Later I saw patients from Java and Japan and we met each other in the common field of universal human conflicts. Basically people are the same and understand each other in their needs.

It is difficult to accept the thought that behind the divergent cultural differences identical hearts beat and the same feelings burn. Communication between disparate groups is difficult because gestures, sounds and words are different. Yet, that is merely the outer aspect of our stereotyped view of different cultural types.

The over-hurried psychologist in us wants all this expressed in precise terms of human behavior He asks rather prematurely: What is the difference between Orient and Occident? What is the psychological motivation behind Confucianism and Buddhism? What deep-seated complex divided Christianity into so many militant denominations, and how can we integrate these contrasts?

The fallacy of describing psychological differences between East and West is that we tend to interpret them as contrasts rather than as a more or less pronounced variant of universal human qualities.

The Oriental ideal of man is in the first place that of oneness, of being *one* with the family, one with the fatherland, one with the cosmos, one with Nirvana. The Eastern psyche looks for a direct aesthetic contact with reality through the help of an undefinable empathy and intuition. Eternal truth lies behind reality, behind the veil of Maya. Man is seen as part of the universe, with the ideal of passive servility and submission in non-irritability. His peace is idealized in rest and relaxation, in meditation, in being without manual and mental travail. His happiness lies in the ecstasy of feeling united with the universal cosmos. Asceticism, self-redemption, and poverty are still ideals in Oriental culture.

The Occidental ideal of man is much more individual and distinctive. Man is the rebellious Lucifer, confronting the universe with his own individual ego. He builds up ego defenses behind his mask and manipulates reality aggressively with logical deductions and abstractions. He wants to become independent of his teachers, bypassing them. Only the devoted artist among Western man may reach the ecstasy of creation. But the engineer's compulsion to technical perfectionism may degenerate into the megalomaniacal delusion of atomic destruction.

Mankind will always experience evolution, regression, differentiation, degeneration, and cultural growth. All these forces exist side by side. Today, however, man is able to gather, as an aid to his development, a wealth of psychological, anthropological, sociological, and historical insight which *can* be used in writing future history. *For the first time in history man is able to compare his epoch with the other epochs on the basis of factual historical and social knowledge.* Compare this epoch with the known historical facts at the time of the Vienna peace conference in 1815. Most of the world and its history was still unknown at that fateful conference—which nevertheless brought us nearly 100 years of international stability.

It is possible for human beings to use historical and sociological knowledge in the shaping of their destiny Man's political science is based on this belief. Man shapes his own life even when he repeatedly lets go through inertia and destructive exaltation.

In the period immediately following a war the general mood of mankind is depressive. Vague feelings of guilt, loss, chaos, and destruction contribute to this mood. Accordingly, people seem to be waiting for new catastrophe. They express only the pessimism, the guilt feelings of a war-torn world. However, gradually man grows out of this passive and fatalistic acceptance of life. He becomes more and more aware of the fact that he is a thinking being, capable of creation.

Our historical knowledge does not go back much further than 10,000 years, though man, homo sapiens, had already been on earth about 200,000 years. The economic and individualistic civilization of the human race has existed at most 6,000 years. What we designate as civilization—human training beyond the instincts of animal life and dawn of social consciousness—is a thin, superficial layer of man's pattern of action. Only during a small percentage of his existence has he been practising civilized habits. Thus, we may say in a superficial way that man is about ten per cent civilized, and ninety per cent animal.

We are only at the beginning of man's humanization. We have only begun to break away from our animal-like submission to jungle law. That may explain why we can so easily lose the veneer of civilization and once more behave like Neanderthalers.

But progress has been made, even though it has proved difficult to control man's destructive spirit. Looking at man psychologically, it seems miraculous that he has even now been able to form as peaceful and well-organized a community as he has.

Aggressive, competitive twentieth-century man has a better opportunity to become civilized and to form a permanent culture than man at any time before him. Moral training, through modern education, can bring human instincts of destruction and aggression under control. In spite of such bestial regressions as Hitler's systematized criminalization of his followers, man has proved that he is capable of forming peaceful and stable communities. His need for dependency and his social needs force him to accept, no matter what the cost, the difficult and restrictive rules of his community.

Yet, there is danger in over-emphasizing community ties Bureaucratic planners, for instance, can have an inhibiting effect on human spontaneity and creativity. We have to be very careful with the selection of those who administer and govern us. They are those who finally touch the push-buttons. We have to be aware, too, how easily a power-loaded bureaucracy can show inner decay and promote the reign of aggressive morons. Nevertheless, the baffling hurdles that have to be taken can gradually help us to sublimate aggression and to turn the spirit of revolt within the mind into productive cooperation. Dictatorial governments, however, suppress the tolerance for these little inconveniences and so may arouse greater aggression in the end. Psychological experiments with cats and rats, for instance, have proved that even instinctively hostile animals can be taught to live in peaceful collaboration.

Civilization affords man the opportunity of raising his cultural level through interrelation, confluence, diffusion, and the simple process of cultural osmosis. In isolated cultures, primitive forms of thinking have a greater tendency to become dominant; this we see in the study of group delusions and contagious mass psychoses. But contact with other mentalities *forces* speculation upon and criticism of one's own limited intellectual and cultural matters.

Thoughts and mentalities need marriage and diffusion, a mental conjugation. All propaganda for racial and spiritual purity and isolation aims at sterility and death. Races also die of old age. Mental autocracy is just as lethal as its economic counterpart. Collective training toward continually perfecting human endeavor is the quintessence of civilization.

Civilization and its stabilization into a culture depend on a continuity of the mind. It is a precarious mental adventure, requiring constant alertness. When alertness declines, the material and mental roots of culture dissolve, traditions disappear, and creation is halted. Nevertheless, the latent spirit of past civilizations may speak to us from its creative monuments, the symbols from the past.

Isolated civilizations are hardly to be found any more, and modern historical and anthropological studies point to a continuity of civilizations through their contact with one another. Iron curtains cannot prevent such exchange. *Psychology teaches that even negative, hostile contact exerts a challenging influence.* Mutual suggestion acts directly but also paradoxically. Victim and aggressor are psychologically united. Unknowingly they identify with each other and take over each other's habits.

Civilization asks real devotion of its creators. When the creative minds that form a civilization cease to work and struggle for their ideals, civilization is lost.

As said before, it is often because of the burden of his very civilization that man is neurotic, for neurosis is the result of conflict between the instincts' demands for expression and fulfillment and civilization's demand that these demands be suppressed and restricted. Such neurosis is the toll we must pay for further humanization. The human being is an ambivalent animal with both a love of culture and a hatred of civilization. Man is always feeling his way between different dangers until he finds the golden middle road. He is always fighting a number of battles—though he's not always aware of them—till he understands them and so comes to control them better. Although he cannot stem the tide, he can always channel it.

Man is neurotic, but he is *not* more neurotic today than he was in the past. The man of the Middle Ages was deeply burdened with fears, hysteria, hallucinations. He lived in a world of witches and werewolves. Our Victorian grandparents were raised in an age of dull frustration and stiff tradition. They dreamed their lives away in meaningless Weltschmerz and melancholy.

Indeed, modern man, for all his show-window personality and cold superficiality, is mentally healthier, more alert, and better adjusted to his "man-made" environment than were his ancestors. True, he is distressed because of his greater awareness of inner turbulence, and he suffers more—temporarily—with his new knowledge. But it is healthier to suffer consciously and accept the challenge of a new insight than to pay the dull price of lifelong frustrations endured because of dogma, taboo, and persecution by tradition. And, paradoxically, it is through this very neurotic battle that man will find his way to a better plane of living which he reaches through change of hidden forces in him. No strength without pain!

In his battle for security and serenity man must first learn to endure insecurity and uncertainty. It is the same with his battle for universal justice. *Only when he is very consciously able to suffer and tolerate personal injustice will he be able to champion a movement promoting justice for others. But as long as his battle for justice is rooted in self-pity and a personal feeling of misery, no justice for others will be attained.*

When we speak of our neurotic world we imply that people suffer nowadays from inner paradoxes, and from an awareness of the contrasting forces and motivations acting on them. Yet this very doubt can help them to become less dogmatic, less satisfied with their little strategic solutions. They will see their way to exchanging mechanical perfectionism for free creativity. The conscious choice between political extremes seems a difficult one because it requires honesty, not corrupted by either emotional histrionics or pedantic social theories. And then, suddenly, man discovers that the contrasts belong together as part of one immense polarity.

We must distinguish between man's *contrasting inner forces* and a passive cultural *"horizontalism"* aiming at limited goals of adjustment and security. Cultural "horizontalism" is leveling and vulgarizing. But alert, continual awareness of man's limitations and turbulent inner paradoxes challenges man's creativity. Horizontalism creates passive onlookers and bystanders. People, deprived of responsibility, become incapable of mental initiative or moral action. They are transformed into the shouting crowds at sports events or the cheering masses guided by totalitarian propaganda.

Nineteenth-century European civilization, although seemingly stable, was too smug, too sure and secure about itself, too comfortable for the few, too brutally competitive for the many. Men lived from it, but did not provide for it, and it became a perversion of civilization, a semi-culture. It was devoured from within.

Contemporary civilization is growing more complex by the day and seems even chaotic. Earthly goods are still divided unequally, creating a breeding ground for social struggle, scapegoatism, racism. The idol of technical production created the big metropolis, where man got lost in material competition. Now men feel naked and undefended; they tend to hide more and more in great cities for protection against loneliness and fear. Thus they cut themselves off from the inspiring challenge nature offers. Scientific techniques may put dangerous powers in the hands of incompetents: automobiles in the hands of aggressive neurotics, atomic bombs in the hands of political adventurers. Sports, films, dancing, and sex have become drugs offering artificial ecstasy and cheap intoxication—camouflage for empty lives. Sex is looked upon more often as a hungry need than an erotic art. Shallow education may inflate men by providing empty factual knowledge without emotional foundation, making them into intellectual accumulations of facts without experience. Our schools too often serve more as fact-factories than as training centers for individual thinking. Men are still so undecided about their own goals that any outside influence—whether a Stalin or a "yellow" newspaper columnist—can push their minds into some temporary malpractice. There is a general lack of awareness of these influences.

The veneration and over-evaluation of technique and material production covers up man's ever-present enervating and weakening need for security. Like the dictator, technique requires an infantile, servile attitude from people. The need for security increases our passivity and moral cowardice. The ancient myths cannot soothe mankind any more. Today, the myth of a perfect technocracy is replacing the older myths of powerful, protective idols. In urban culture, where people are always kept busy even during leisure time, the challenge to face the hard forces of nature outside and the subtle forces of instinct within us is hardly ever met. Only confrontation with these two forces can form sound character and personality. We have to turn the systematic breeding of dissatisfaction—as stimulated and suggested by technological production—into greater awareness of the processes going on inside man's mind.

Overpopulation and increasing inter-human rivalry

Since the science of hygiene and medical prophylaxis has prolonged the mean age of man, so that death and disease no longer regulate and limit the growth of our population, the world has had to adjust to new problems. Statistical life expectancy has risen with startling swiftness. In ancient Greece it was 29 years; by 1900 it had moved upward to 44 years, today it has risen to 62 years. For women this expectancy is even greater, implying special problems for them.

Statistics tell us that 32 per cent of all married women are widowed by the age of 60, and 55 per cent by the age of 64, because of greater mortality among older men. Beyond the age of 64, more than two-thirds of all women in the United States are either widowed or unmarried. Even so quick a glance at statistics as this points to a forced deprivation of love relations. The old-aged are compelled to live alone in a period of their life in which they become more dependent and in need of help.

In other countries we see that the increasing overpopulation threatens the possibility of providing food and work for all inhabitants. In some such overpopulated countries as Holland and Japan, we find that the governments, forced by emergency, are trying to handle a guided emigration to less populated countries. In underdeveloped countries, the help of medical scientists is asked. In order to prevent future overpopulation, planned parenthood is recommended.

But there are also less obvious implications of overpopulation. Planned parenthood is not enough, certain forms of living have created new demands on mental hygiene. We have become aware that the tendency toward urbanization and anarchic suburbanism provokes bewildering psychic problems in both metropolis and suburbia. Town planners and nature lovers are posing the question of how to bring the challenge and the influence of nature back to the homes without transforming the country and its highways into one big girdle of suburban monotony.

Overpopulation also creates a universal trend toward mass-criteria. It creates an illusion of quantity while overlooking the qualitative improvement of man and mankind.

The core of the question is that the threatening overpopulation and the disappearance of open spaces on our planet have brought our world into a new phase of development. This new phase forces people more than ever to cooperate and literally to co-exist where they could originally "go West," explore new regions and seek for new adventure.

Human rivalry is not bred between siblings only, but has become an overwhelming problem in the world at large. *The science of mutual tolerance has become more needed than ever!* No destructive genocide, no hyperatomic war with its millions of deaths, can destroy so much of earth's population that it checks, albeit in a murderous and cynical way, this new biological fact of overpopulation and expanding mankind. *World War II, with its loss of nearly 30 million lives, made only a small dent in the statistical trend upward.*

True, man's rivalry and mutual hatred can be shown in many social symptoms. There is sibling rivalry, class consciousness and national competition; there is the spread of mutual prejudice and of racialism. Mankind has created many "isms" to shape the delusion that men cannot possibly tolerate one another. How easy to appeal to dark destructive forces by selling cheap promises of a glorious future! But the rivaling forces in the world have to learn the challenge of fair competition. Future psychology will have as its most provoking task that of teaching people to tolerate and understand each other.

In ancient Greece, wars were interrupted when the time of the Olympic Games drew near. People are able to stop their competitive and aggressive behavior the moment they are inspired by a greater aim than that of immediate local chauvinism.

Man, the "dreamer-fighter," will gradually learn to recognize and adapt himself not only to dangers from the outside world but also to the cruel hostile fantasies of intolerance coming from inside. His inner dangers are his conscious and unconscious fantasies about the world, his overpowering instinctual drives, his fury, his cruel dreams. Most of these fantasies are lent to or imprinted on him by communal traditions, myths and fantasies, causing man to live continually in a state of preparedness and alert under a constant burden of fear.

Can we adjust and reconcile people to a rapidly changing world? Did Pandora unleash forces man can no longer control?

Clinical psychology is astutely aware of the fact that insight, knowledge, and the will to face problems have in themselves a curative and regenerative action. Mutual insight diminishes tension. It teaches people to live with their limitations and to accept their ignorance.

Unawareness of inward fears and panic breeds passive escapists, who consequently surrender to their doom in a mood of destructive fatalism. Perhaps the biggest psychological battle we have to fight is against such mental apathy, passivity and self-pity, as is proved by the study of panic and fear in man.

A free democratic world finds its own answers to problems by building up through trial and error various legal and institutional controls, protecting society against its own foibles and failures.

At this very moment mankind knows enough about itself and its history, about man and the natural, social and intrapsychic factors guiding him, to be able to plan its future tentatively with scientific and philosophic wisdom and leadership.

Yet, such intelligent leadership has to be cultivated in small, selected teams, fortified by an inner wisdom as well as the critical knowledge that their very planning can breed the germ of new danger in that it may kill the spontaneity of higher wisdom. Such a leading group has to teach the world how to convert the manifold "isms," "principles" and "ideologies" into the patient wisdom of repetitious tactics and probable compromises. And let them not forget that the reasonable man is a lonely man. He cannot be too gregarious, since he must constantly defend his individual integrity.

The new Atomic Age has put before us enormous new challenges, asking of man unfamiliar forms of awareness in order to check the tremendous outer and inner forces which he has unleashed.

The contrast

When the world received the momentous news of the first dropping of an atomic bomb and the surrender of Japan, I was in tropical Surinam, Netherlands Guiana, north of Brazil. I was there to talk about welfare and first aid to be provided for the mother country, and to investigate political internees who lived in a jungle camp. Our car radio picked up the news as we drove the long dusty road from the internment camp in the jungle back to Paramaribo. The government had asked me to advise it about the camp inhabitants who had been detained there for political reasons, for collaboration with the enemy, rebellion, refusal to go into the army, and so on. Most of the inmates had in some way directed their private grudges and resentments against their fatherland. It was rather depressing work because in several cases trouble could have been prevented. The harsh treatment they received would have been unnecessary if they had been treated originally in a more adept psychological way.

The dramatic radio report disclosed news of the end of the Second World War, and various kinds of local festivities were announced. But I was in a strange frame of mind. The thought of the one hundred thousand people killed by a bomb at one and the same time was to play a role in my feeling and thinking for a long time to come. I knew the danger of too much horror. *The boredom of repetitious sensationalism gradually makes people surrender to the idea. Gradually they lose all sense of values and do not see tremendous peril and the danger signals. They finally accept doom and destruction as the only way out.*

Rumors about new and horrible explosives had been circulating since the beginning of the war. In Occupied Holland I continually had to deal with these rumors and realities. The Germans had proudly announced a new secret weapon as their greatest discovery. Our own chemical engineers had talked about the mysterious announcements in the most fantastic terms. And later, after my escape in 1942, I had been able to report to Allied authorities the psychological influence of this mixture of rumor and reality. There had been a terrible fear that the Germans would be ready first with the new tremendous weapons. Now we knew that the Allies had won the race in the technical application of what had been a theoretical possibility.

Our jungle road through Guiana, especially built to transport bauxite (an aluminum ore) from the heart of the jungle to the harbor, wound past virgin tropical forest. The dust of the road mingles with that peculiar mixture of delicate fragrance of flowers and the acrid odor of decaying roots and leaves. From time to time we passed a bush-Negro village. My mind went back a day or so when we had met a few Chavanne Indians from the Amazon jungle on the same spot. They had come downstream to exchange some of their products. Theirs was a beautiful, strong race with simple habits. We knew from experience that contact with a "higher" culture would soon bring about a degeneration of their habits. They would come into contact with alcohol and tuberculosis, with competitiveness and lust for power, all of which would ruin their customs and their lives.

That tremendous contrast between a simple culture and the technical over-sophistication of our society remained in my mind. On one side were men from the archaic past without technical knowledge, living in a primitive community, completely adjusted to its surroundings; on the other side was modern man, the eternally dissatisfied conqueror who had achieved the peak of his potentialities—a bomb capable of stupendous destruction.

And in my mind there was a distinct resemblance between the acrid odor of tropical decay and the atomic explosion. Day after day, driving along that sun-scorched road, I meditated compulsively on that one moment in time that took the lives of one hundred thousand people. What is the sense of such a fate for the guilty and the innocent alike who find a sudden common grave? What is the meaning of life if it is that cheap, that easy to destroy? The jeep, bouncing along the hot jungle road, made agonizing sounds, and the daily trip took on a nightmarish quality. And every night, as I wrote long reports about my rebellious and psychopathic fellow men, weighing the pros and cons of their dissension or treachery, I was aware that far off, one push of a button had destroyed a city.

It was only much later that I realized how this, my first impression of mass-atomization, made a cynic out of me to cover my hurt ideals about mankind. For years I repressed my fears and disillusionment until gradually the awareness awoke that the stupendous bomb forced us into a new age with a new loyalty. Man's loyalty had suddenly to expand from his cherished own nation and fatherland to mankind as a whole. But how difficult this is to swallow for those entangled in private feuds, chauvinistic prejudices and ideological preoccupations!

The shadow of the mushroom

Forgive me for repeating here part of the frightening reality of atomic warfare. But it is the frightening impact that makes the scientists so divided among each other and about the moral implications of what they have to say to mankind. The impact of the bomb on mankind and its history is much more a socio-psychological problem than a physical one.

We are so well acquainted with the mushroom image rising upward after the detonation that it is already difficult to realize that with the Bikini type of H-bomb, more than a million tons of material are sucked up from the earth toward the top of the mushroom into the stratosphere. This pulverized earth forms a threatening umbrella extending 200 miles across the earth. The result—besides the immediate destruction of every living thing on earth within a radius of 3½ miles—is that radioactive isotopes are liberated, some of which (like carbon-14) may have a lifetime of 5600 years. After the explosion, the radioactivity of the mushroom is estimated as equal to 800,000 tons of radium, and a year later, equal to 100 tons of radium. A bomb like the one exploded at Bikini Atoll on March 1, 1954, would make an area of several thousand square miles dangerous to life for a long time.

This continual radiation may be called the "creeping suicide" of mankind. Man has become the guinea pig of new and very involved physical experiments. According to the geneticist and Nobel prize winner Professor H. J. Muller,[1] there will be a positive chance of harmful hereditary mutations in the population. The danger to heredity may not be apparent for several years, but then it will leave in its wake abortion, degeneration, malformation, and increased cancer incidence. The continual danger from radiation is great: it may wipe out mankind in 1000 years. Even the tests carried out with atomic bombs have already increased some radiation in the atmosphere. In the summer of 1955 the radiation received by the average American was as much as is received from a chest X-ray (one tenth of a roentgen unit). Geneticists predict that one unit will take away around 5 days of your life. The Japanese fisherman who were 80 miles distant from the Bikini explosion received between 200 and 500 roentgen units. Twenty-five roentgen units is generally looked upon as over-exposure and may cause radiation sickness. Physicist Ralph E. Lapp also warned against the residual radiation coming from lethal radioactive fallout in localized areas.

Strontium-90, cesium-137, and carbon-14, all by-products of the nuclear blast, are long-lived radioactive elements produced by atomic explosions into the atmosphere. They will then gradually penetrate the organs—via food and inhalation—to provoke destruction and hereditary change. Every atom of strontium we ingest will remain in our skeleton while giving off, 24 hours a day, beta radiation for its half life of 35 years. The fission products will be absorbed slowly in the bones and other organs, and replace the calcium of the bone tissue—most probably causing leukemia and cancer in its wake. At this moment, thanks to the atomic experimentation, 65 megatons have already increased the radiation hazard and burdened the atmosphere of Mother Earth with an equivalent of 100 pounds of strontium-90. (*Scientific American,* Vol. 20, June 1959.) When it rains, fallout from nuclear blasts is washed down the ground. A number of youngsters of the next generation will probably be maimed. The strontium units in the bones of youngsters have already increased and many a scientist expects the absorption to increase in the future. Some predict, as a result of continued fallout, that in 1966 ten times the amount of strontium-90 will be accumulated in the bones of children (*Science News Letter,* May 23, June 13, 1959 and April 16, 1960); people all over the world will suffer death and illness from the nuclear tests conducted to date.

Yet, we have not finished with the possible physical harm that could be done apart from the incidence of full-fledged atomic war. The tremendous dust explosion of the Krakatao crater in the East Indies in 1883 decreased the intensity of the radiation of the sun, changed the temperature of the earth, and in its wake the melting of the earth's icecap. Atomic dust may do the same because the mushroom acts like an atmospheric screen and filter. Atomic dust, furthermore, forms saltpeter acid in the atmosphere, with deleterious results for all living things, animal and plant alike. Increased condensation may disturb weather and the rain pattern.

All this atomic news is regularly piped into the different channels of information. Some scientists agree with the dire forecasts, others do not. Yet the news has aroused a vague feeling of unrest which most people immediately repress to disguise their fears. They don't want to know and don't want to become aware of mankind's new guinea-pig state. A fear too great is no longer comprehended. We psychiatrists, however, come across these hidden thoughts in the dreams of patients, in their private silent panics and in the wish not to talk about the subject any more. The fact of the matter is that for the first time in world history man can "play" with subtle equilibriums in the universe without being aware what he will disturb. For instance, what will an atom bomb do when it reaches the moon? What is the human wrench doing to a subtle celestial equilibrium? This problem of nuclear ecology has become just as problematic as human ecology: e.g., the disorders we shape in breaking social equilibriums.

Originally the bomb gave the world a moral shock, and the vision of 100,000 victims was burned into our consciences for a long time. The past ten or fifteen years has been a period when people expected atomic warfare to erupt momentarily—and some are surprised (indeed, disappointed!) that this did not take place during crises now almost forgotten—Azerbaidzhan, Matsu, Berlin, Israel, Hungary, etc. It hasn't happened, and today's crisis is not very much more likely to end in direct atomic warfare than did yesterday's. Man, however, grows used to horror and danger. Atomic weapons information is no longer on the first page of our newspapers—only the picture of the mushroom, the new visual euphemism for hell and holocaust. This impression from the front page of our thinking is the great danger, because in the meantime the storehouse of weapons has grown larger, and people don't think in terms of prevention of Armageddon anymore.

The H-bomb has given a new responsibility to the world, a

new superconscience, the responsibility for the physical and mental health of future generations. As man becomes more aware that he can shape his own fate, he also learns that he can destroy his world. How utterly difficult it is for man to conceive of a responsibility extending beyond his own lifetime. In the epoch in which we live we have the responsibility not merely for ourselves and our children, but, together with our enemies, we have to shoulder responsibility for Mother Earth and her future generations. "*Après nous le déluge*" has become too dangerously cynical. Man must now accept the challenge of looking at his world beyond his own time. What a challenge and how difficult to conceive! Responsibility means responsibility to one's self and one's own conscience. How is this possible in a world with growing tendencies toward conformity and totalitarian concepts? We repeat: the answer is that man at this moment of his development has reached the point where he is able to write his own history.

The paradox of peace and aggression

Human solidarity and hostility maintain at this moment an uneasy balance. The smaller the community, the greater the sense of solidarity. How many men are really moved by war or tremendous destruction on the other side of the world? Not until war knocks directly at our very doors and threatens us and our soldiers do we wake up. If the planet Mars were to wage war against Earth, solidarity among the nations would at once become a reality.

The word *peace* is related to the Sanskrit root *pac* = to bind. We find this meaning back in our word pact, the binding mutual agreement. To pay, paccare, means to appease those to whom you are indebted. The German word Frieden (vrede in Dutch) expresses more the passive connotation of being secure and protected.

As a binding pact in all religions and social systems, one finds in astonishingly similar form the same golden rule: *Do naught unto others which would cause you pain if done to you.*

Peace is war against aggressive hostile impulses—war is escape from the more subtle involvements and tensions of peace. I had never realized the paradoxical implications of peace quite so clearly as I did after my experiences with those camp inmates I had to judge, who incessantly fought their private battles and harbored grudges against society.

A great deal of so-called peace is not necessarily as peaceful as the fervent lover of peace presumes. Important are the inner motives, the realization of the warring contrasts in man, and the spiritual background of the condition we call "peace." Peace can be the very mask of aggression, and aggression the disguise of a peaceful mind. Perpetual armistice is possible between people—a constant state of unsolved tension, which erroneously is called peace. I've known so-called "peaceful" lovers, silent mates in marriage, who avoided every complication and conflict and thus every fruitful solution of controversies by escaping into tacit peacefulness. Among the naive advocates of world peace, I know some who radiate aggression, who are white-hot with rage and the lust to fight the warmongers! Many a fanatical pacifist is merely fighting his own unsolved hostile tendencies.

Before the war, a case of overt hostile behavior had kept me busy for many months. This patient was a girl. She had an excellent job, but her heart was full of wrath and she experienced an inner sense of crisis. She had come to me because she felt depressed and had crying spells. Her only complaint at the time, however, was that her body had ceased to function normally. She had many psychosomatic complaints. Her body was aching and she could not eat. We gradually discovered that there had been too great a loneliness in her life—loneliness, ambition, and lack of love. Overwhelmed with bitterness toward the people around her, she finally felt so lost and cold that mental anguish had led her to my office.

After several months of difficult collaboration and exploration, I was able to unravel many of her pseudo-aggressions and jabbing criticisms. But when she began to discern the artificial barrier she had thrown up around her infantile sensitivity, her resentment increased. She became more sensitive and vulnerable, and did not quite know how to handle her once protective hostilities. Meanwhile one of her friends asked her to give shelter to a refugee child, a little girl. In former days she would never have done this, but now she agreed because it was an emergency. Sarcastically she explained that she did not decide to care for the child because of pity or love but only as a protest against certain political tendencies in Central Europe, which she hated. She probably did it also to please her doctor, but no word was said about that.

For the child, this was by no means a happy situation, though she took my patient's tantrums remarkably well. The arrangement was, nevertheless, torture to both of them.

Two events, however, changed my patient completely. Her little guest became ill and, as it happened, I fell ill at the same time. When she came to see me after my recuperation, she tried to discover what hidden motives had made me, the doctor, seek refuge in physical illness. In the course of her subtle questioning she began to ask herself the same kind of questions about the child. And gradually she discovered that in this case she herself had been the one to blame. Out of guilt, her pent-up longing for tenderness was awakened; she became more kindly toward the child and friendlier to people in general, though she still had trouble keeping her hostile defenses in check. There are those who resent any form of affection so long as they feel that it makes them dependent on someone. However, the moment they are able to correct their megalomanic need for loneliness—which they unconsciously translate into power—their capacity for loving breaks through.

Whenever my patient appeared for treatment thereafter, she surprised me with a number of adroit psychological observations of the child and her office colleagues. Still resisting intrusion by me, the stranger, she did not once mention her own inner troubles. She began to read psychological essays and attended a popular lecture course given by a well-known psychologist.

Then one day I received a letter in which she explained that she did not need to see me again, that she had recovered her peace of mind, and that much of her animosity had turned into love for the child who had miraculously come her way. In a final paragraph she let me have it! "You are just as aggressive and hostile as I am, but you work off your aggression by piercing the minds of your poor victims with psychological arrows."

This abrupt ending to the case was a little hard to swallow. Her last remark injured my pride. Not until I had gone through war and the Nazi occupation did I realize for myself how much inner aggression and hostility can be converted into sharp psychological sophistication. And authors writing about peace have to be just as wary of their paradoxical statements. Are they shooting verbal arrows disguised by felicitous concern at innocent readers, or is peace among men really their aim?

We hate and we like destruction

Before we investigate the positive actions we can take against the atomic peril and atomic fear, we have to be deeply aware of man's contrasting attitudes toward danger and catastrophe. There is a tragic side to our personalities which accounts for our unconscious readiness to engage in war. Consciously—and truthfully—we say we hate war, we hate death and destruction. But deeply rooted in each of us is a primitive urge—a submerged personality level—that finds satisfaction in war's terrible destruction; indeed, it craves such a nemesis.

I remember a lecture I gave before a group of ultra-pacifists years before the outbreak of the Second World War. These pacifists thought they might still be able to prevent war. All sorts of idealistic actions were planned, and the aid of leading statesmen from different countries was recruited. "Moral Rearmament" was the slogan at that time. I warned my audience as emphatically as I could that they should not assume a passive attitude toward the political evils in the center of Europe. I pointed out that Hitler was trying to misuse the European pacifist movements to weaken the more militant anti-Nazi movements in the countries surrounding Germany, knowing, cynically, that the pacifism of the one might activate and fortify the aggressive potency of the other. Pacifism in our country might activate the potential enemy at the other side of the frontier, I said. Even in people who profess pacifism, deep aggressive and destructive drives have by no means disappeared, although they may have been channeled into more acceptable expressions of human action.

When I had finished, the pacifistic lambs had turned into most violent wolves. It was as if their pent-up hatred and aggression had been released and was now directed at me. I was almost thrown out. They themselves proved that they still nurtured various forms of violence. Unfortunately, some of them later paid the penalty for their misdirected idealism in Hitler's concentration camps.

Man's unconscious expectation of war and Armageddon is dangerous, indeed. It prepares the mind for what is justified as an "inevitable fact." It paves the way for passive surrender to the dreaded event. It is analogous to the thought-process of a thief who feels more secure when he finally surrenders to his pursuers. He cannot bear the growing insecurity of the feeling that he may be caught at any moment. He prefers the security of imprisonment. All of us are in some way the same kind of insecure criminals. Nemesis and downfall can free us from our pent-up primitive drives!

People make use of many pat excuses to justify their hostilities. Consciously we talk about our love for culture and for civilization; we say we love peace and hate destruction. Such is the innate ambivalence in all of us that the destruction we profess to hate may be, at the same time, the very destruction our hidden primitive instincts like and crave.

I remember an acquaintance, a seemingly unpretentious girl. She came from a highly civilized milieu and had an intelligent and scientific mind. During the German Occupation she became a spy for the Nazis, betraying her fatherland and her former ideals of peace and human decency as well. There is no need for me to chronicle here the cruelties and atrocities for which she was responsible. My only point is that hidden aggressive drives such as hers may lie behind the cultural façade of any human being.

We can grow used to wholesale slaughter. After all, the population of the world is far too large ever to make an instantaneous total annihilation of mankind probable. Our primitive fantasy even tells us secretly that we will be among the few who will survive the radioactive dust, leaving us as inheritors of the remnants of the world. The truth is that somewhere in our minds we rather prefer the atomic show, especially when we have been hardened to suffering by fear and intensive war propaganda. Our technical age has insidiously made us much more self-destructive. Speed and motion have replaced feeling and emotion.

The primitive in us enjoys the turmoil of war; it admires the technical dream of human omnipotence and tremendous destruction. I once treated a conscientious objector who refused to carry weapons or wear a uniform. He presented the most ethical justifications for his refusal. After many therapeutic sessions, however, I learned that he had a terrific fear of militaristic symbols. He feared his own unconscious and deeply hidden criminal lust to kill and to destroy. He could not run the risk of carrying a deadly weapon nor of having such a perfect excuse for killing his fellow human beings.

Are we really full of panic about the atom bomb? How many among us are already thinking that we should drop atom bombs before our potential enemies attack us? A number of people daily write to the papers—see almost any "Letters to the Editor" column—to say that they think we should drop the bombs now—first. That was especially true when we smugly thought that the eventual enemy was not ready for reprisals.[2] Thousands of times we have in our dreams blasted away at all whom we hate. Behind the display of horror our primitive megalomaniacal wish for terrible devastation—a childish dream of revengeful omnipotence—is fulfilled. What a powerful gesture! What frustrated magicians we are! Imagine, one push of a button and a whole world may vanish! In our dreams we become as powerful as God. Man is a crazy dreamer. His technical toys fulfill his primitive dreams and compensate for his lack of inner strength and self-confidence. In science fiction we give vent in a romantic way to those primitive magic fantasies.

I once treated a member of a Dutch bomber crew in World War II who repeatedly had the following dream. He dreamed he was flying on a mission to drop a huge bomb on his home town because the enemy had a military installation in one of the main buildings. The sun was going down when he reached his target; he dropped the bomb and started his return trip. On the way back he was afflicted with a strange inner turmoil. Then he saw a huge mountain rising in front of him. But instead of trying to avoid it he directed his plane toward the black mass. He crashed into the mountain—and awoke knowing that in his nightmare he had attempted suicide. He realized that because he inflicted destruction he had to be punished: suicide is the ultimate self-punishment. Later, on one of his real missions, he was killed.

Despite all the scare stories, if the Third World War should come, it would probably not mean direct universal destruction, though we may not be sure of the aftermath of radiation. Men, if they remain living in the same delusion, will try to destroy one another—as they have tried in the past—until only a few remnants of human society remain to begin civilized life over again —to become, let us hope, wiser than we are (if the genetic damage will permit).

Perhaps a future war would not start immediately with rockets and atomic missiles. Yet, the construction of the atomic bomb stockpiles is a truer token of man's inner motivations than all spoken words. We are already in a period of such limited trial-wars as those in Korea and Indo-China. The H-bomb will be kept in abeyance for a more violent phase. War always begins with military pomp: with fleets of war planes and mechanized armies, with all the equipment our armament factories can make. We built them; thus, we have to use them. Perhaps our diplomats will be able to outlaw the atomic bomb as they have outlawed the use of poison gas. If so, then we shall discover another new scientific weapon, one which has not yet been included in the rules of the military game. "Praise the Lord and pass the ammunition!"

However, we are not *only* children and fighting dreamers. Apart from the phrases and the catchwords, we still possess positive, active drives for peace. There are *constructive* drives, too: for thinking, and for building a more harmonious society. But these drives have nothing to do with fear and dread of attack. The compulsion to destroy is not the principal thing that motivates human beings, even though we often behave aggressively and destructively toward one another. Human love and purposefulness and intelligent social adaptation and cooperation exist too. These feelings cannot be regulated or channeled by diplomats, military staffs, or atomic scientists. These positive roots of civilization have nothing to do with the checking of aggressive behavior. International military strategy can only check the aggressive discharges of states and communities in much the same way that our police force tries to check the individual criminals among us. Positive peace, however, is built in a different atmosphere and with different means.

Pacifism and the search for a common moral base

Some people today are certain that the one way to insure peace among men is to play up the tremendous horrors of the next war. Behind this sort of thinking is the notion that to picture the terrific destruction of an atomic war will create so deep a fear in all people that they will actually be persuaded by fear to build a constructive plan for peace.

But we know that people do not entirely abhor carnage and gruesomeness; they experience hidden pleasure even as they shudder. Anyone who sees movies, watches television, or listens to radio programs must be convinced of man's tremendous self-intoxication with destruction. Psychological studies tell us that fear *never* evokes peaceful reactions. On the contrary, people react to fear by preparing themselves instantly for defense and attack. Man reacts to danger and fright by becoming aggressive, not peaceful. After he gets out of his initial paralysis he tries to land the first blow. *Involuntarily,* man in fear looks for a means of counterattack, and by so doing prepares himself for the very fight he dreads so deeply.

This was brought home to me time and again among combat soldiers. The "green" troops indulged in all kinds of philosophical discussions on the "stupidity of war," but when they were really scared, when the enemy attacked, they fought like demons. For many a soldier the free release of aggression became the one ecstatic experience in his life, as if war were the only challenge to man's bravery and courage.

Before the war an idealistic friend of mine in Holland had been a prominent pacifist. He was known as the tireless organizer of a world-wide anti-war movement. After the Nazis invaded the country, however, and he was compelled to live under the daily threat of terror, he became one of the most violent and capable workers in the underground.

Despite all pacifist theory, the urge to defend oneself is easily aroused in man. When it is aroused, cruel lust for retaliation and aggression is also awakened. It is dangerous to unleash these hidden human instincts without being prepared for them. Much of our instinctual control is based on awareness and repeated training in curbing our instincts. Alas, in our culture of daily stimulated dissatisfaction it is difficult to find the noble image of progress. The curbing side of our lives is more emphasized than ecstatic affirmation!

So when we read scare stories about a possible atomic war, about the unspeakable destruction it will cause, about the countless cities that will be turned into rubble, about the millions of casualties that will result, can we be expected to react by becoming so afraid of war that in self-defense we will outlaw it? I say no. We are afraid, true; but as soon as we become afraid we begin inwardly to mobilize ourselves for attack. Thus each of these scare stories leads us a little farther along the road to the acceptance of the atomic holocaust of a Third World War. And the culmination of these scares unwittingly builds up the primitive lust to fight, with its attraction of horror and terror lurking in each of us and waiting only to be discharged again. It costs us a lot of energy to keep our instincts under control.

History has shown us many times that war is not an unavoidable fate, and that hostility and aggression can be handled intelligently in a well-planned society. Hungary in the nineteenth century, Norway at the beginning of our century have been examples of this; the peaceful solution of the colonial tie between

India and Great Britain is one of the more recent illustrious examples.

When individual drives are not in harmony, an integrative mental cure is necessary and possible. The same is true of group or state tendencies. *In the future, serious, informed practitioners of social psychology are going to be forced to leave their desks and classrooms and go out into society to influence people in actual social groups.* When they have helped mankind to recognize war as a curable discharge of frustrated instinctual, economic, and political tendencies of the masses, then therapeutic measures can be taken and peace re-established.

Intellect develops slowly. But there is hope for the human being if he will only grow toward greater awareness before an atomic war has annihilated our civilization.

Modern civilization has enough intelligent men to make it a partially planned society, without crises and convulsions, political deceit and unlimited aggression. We are potentially capable of this, but we still must fashion the psychological tools of information and learning, the diplomatic checks and international regulations. The human being, though limited by his physical frontiers, can be conscious of his own evolution; he can grasp the modern tools of his civilization, and with them build a world-embracing community with freedom for all varieties of thought.

To speak of such a basic community is not to speak of a Utopia. But if it is not possible to build such a community, then tensions, aggressions, and greater destruction will spread until the apocalyptic moment of the world's final doom.

The ancient Christian principles of the Congress of Vienna, as we've said, ruled Europe's foreign relations in relative peace from 1815 to 1914. There were a few small wars; there were barbarism, cynicism, and poverty—yet there was still a common moral base, a glimpse of unity. Mutual rapport and communication, therefore, was possible, and led to the creation of some durable treaties.

The modern world has no common moral base. Each country, in justification of its deeds, speaks a different moral language. In World War II we did not even find an acceptable pretext of morality; it was a war *against* something—against Hitler and Mussolini, against Nazism and Fascism. It was not a war *for* anything.

A re-evaluation of moral values does command attention. The "Declaration of Human Rights" as formulated by the United Nations has tried to supply such common values. However, in place of a common moral faith, we have rival ideologies: Marxism, fascism, totalitarianism, capitalism, liberalism, democracy, etc. Often these terms are used more to cover up private politics than to express well-formulated political ideas; they hardly ever express anything with semantic clarity. Historical *materialism* has become the voiced justification and disguising ideology for defense of one-sided totalitarian interests; so-called *idealism* can often be a disguise to perpetuate the old conservative ideas.

Long, sophisticated words, purporting to describe different ideologies, are often used to hide the realities behind them. The words merely cover up mythical concepts. Most of those who talk about Marxism do not know what Marxism is. To recognize mythological wishful thinking for what it really is, this conceptual deceit must be worked out and repeatedly shown to people. One hears, for instance, talk of a Third World War—Russia against America. But "Russia" is a collective myth, and so is America. People in these countries are not basically different. Those who are cheered by or those who suffer from the idea of a future war don't understand their own feelings.

In psychological terms we may say: *Dark myth against dark myth makes for war; the deep unconscious complexes of hidden drives and the absence of clear insights impel man to war.* The destructive but hypnotizing myth itself is created by the propaganda machine of the few who are in charge. If a Third World War breaks loose, it will be a war of warped ideologies, of fantastic myths that do not deal with the reality of human beings who are suffering and dying for it.

Is it possible to establish a common moral basis for all nations? Is it possible to make every nation a loyal member of a universal United Nations? Without such a moral basis it is useless to expect anything but misunderstanding to grow out of world conferences.

A common base is only possible when men are freed of their suspicions and fears, when the masses can be sure of certain economic minimums. The new civilization must have a broad material and psychological basis, spread evenly among the common people of the world, and a common moral basis as well. I hope fervently that the Declaration of Human Rights as formulated by the United Nations may gradually embody such a basic principle.

II

> *By all means let the machine clean our boots and fill our larders, but not our dreams. The five chairs of your necessity shall be made by a machine but not the sixth—make it for your own pleasure. Type your circulars, and keep a pen for your love letters. The machine can give you leisure and dignity for personal relations and the old theme of the heart of man.* (Hsia Ch'ien, "The Dragon Beards versus the Blue Prints.")

The world in the future will witness a tremendous battle between technology and applied understanding of man, between the implied dictatorship of pre-designed, mechanized living and the freedom of creative intellect. In a purely technological world, everybody would become a card in an index file, a card perhaps covered with labels and diplomas, but still a passive part of a metric system. The paradox of actual technique is that gradually the well-being of the machine is valued more highly than the well-being of man.

The struggle against a merely technological civilization will be difficult. It is the struggle against serfdom to machines. Every civilization, including the ancient ones, has tried, after a period of free development, to stabilize itself in rigid institutional forms, has attempted to deny the continual urge toward growth and the transformation to a higher level. Our actual veneration of technique illustrates our practice of turning knowledge into power rather than wisdom.

The future struggle between one-sided technology and humanity will be tremendously important. In our epoch of civilization the science of human behavior must liberate itself from all kinds of tradition, political dogma, and mythical social conceptions before it can take its rightful place in the world. If man can be made to understand that his society, with its rigid codes and stratifications, is in a confused infancy rather than at the apex of its development, if he can be made to understand that the conflicts and contradictions of society can only be resolved by scientific long-range and intelligent social planning, then he will succeed in maintaining what civilization he already has. And he will drive onward toward a greater culture. By "planning" I mean not only economic planning but also planning for freedom and moral guidance beyond our basic limitations.

Much will depend on our future social scientists in cooperation with our great moral leaders, and on the influence they can exert, for they, in the end, will have to present the solutions. Today social scientists are still in their Middle Ages; they are alchemists and sorcerers. Their grand task is to find the natural laws of human behavior independent of ideologies and wishful thinking. But in the sciences of human behavior at this moment there is no unity of principle, no unity of terms.

We are desperately in need of social and psychological scientists today despite the fact that we are still in a phase of history that is reluctant to listen to them. But the time is coming when there will be a united social science with a simple, easily understandable language. It will embrace history, economics, sociology, history, political science, and psychology. At future peace conferences something better than a political or accidental selection of representatives will compose that body. The verbal struggle among the diplomats with its wake of semantic confusion will be replaced by intelligent discussions among experts who know the minds of men.

Revolutions cannot be forced and cannot be suppressed. They arise when men discard a quantity of confusing old beliefs for a new quality of common insight. When the burden of a society reaches a saturation point, a new, often sudden crystallization begins. Every process of growth and evolution implies these convulsions. We now live in a spasm of civilization. That part of civilization will prevail and take control which is able to rejuvenate itself.

Such a revolution of ideas never takes form in "the masses." It originates in those unique leading personalities who fascinate and stimulate the enthusiasm of the common people. These guiding personalities can be either the ideological pathetic seducers or the intelligent masters of human history.

Biology shows us that behind every destruction of life we also observe new life germinating. We live in a universe of innumerable possibilities of growth and regeneration. In spite of his history, man struggles to pull himself aloft, to rise to the tremendous spiritual challenge of the world. We are not a dying civilization. We are still struggling and growing.

What, again, are the positive forces for peace? Let us accept the fact that constructive peace has nothing to do with escape from fear, or prevention of attack. Peace and harmony, equilibrium of the mind, are states resulting from man's highest mental development. More than once in the past man has been able to bring about a harmonious equilibrium among formerly competing forces. We *can* keep the massive aggressive human instinct under control, just as the law can keep criminal and destructive drives of the individual under control.

The answer to how to build a positive peace *cannot* be found in military strategy and atomic science. We cannot let those experts gamble with terrifying forces without having the ultimate wisdom of self-knowledge. Such strategic solutions of world peace always turn into a vicious cycle of defense, aggression, and renewed attack. To resist force inspires more force. Mobilization of armies in one country means counter-mobilization of armies elsewhere. This is a psychological law. Making a trial peace without fear and suspicion promote further peace. That is the other aspect of the same psychological law.

When are we going to be daring enough to use this knowledge of man, and to trust more and more in the constructive aspects of the human mind—more so than our enemies? Who dares to have the force to trust his enemy? This cannot be done without trusting oneself.

We are all displaced persons now because we live in a rapidly changing world. We live in the atomic age and so must choose between constant fear and panic on the one hand, or the acceptance of the challenge of new construction in an ever searching but preferable insecurity, on the other. We have to choose the insecurity of peace over the certainty of destruction and war.

Our fears and inner aggressions unwittingly approve of atomic weapons and the solution of problems by power rather than by a solution attained through wisdom. That is why so many people expect a new war in the near future. Nevertheless, we can also draw upon the civilizing drives within us. And these civilized drives must be relied upon to counteract our primitive wishes to attack and to destroy. The more we can delay a final atomic clash the more time we have to build up the positive forces in the world.

Modern mental science can indicate how to keep human instincts under control, how to mobilize the spirit of goodwill and the honest desire for decency which mankind possesses.

It is the primitive dreamer in us who likes war: appeal to fear, and you press this dreamer to strike back. Our slowly developing humanity has to evolve beyond that primitive phase; it has to construct positive forces for peace.

Now we must all decide in an ultra-conscious way what our future will be. This future is in the hands of the harmonious self-conscious and self-confident man. It is up to every individual being to work toward this aim—of becoming an alert self-aware being, who takes part in the tremendous psychic battle that is going on in the world—or he can let go and evade the issue looking passively and ironically to what others try to do for him. However, nobody *has* to commit suicide. It can always be prevented at the very last moment.

CHAPTER SIX

Psychological Peacefare—The Forgotten Science

The true purpose of psychology and especially its mental-health branch is to free man from his internal tensions by helping him to understand what causes them. Psychology seeks to liberate the human spirit from its dependence on immature thinking so that each man can realize his own potentialities. Psychology teaches man to communicate freely and to express himself, unhampered by prejudices and taboos. It seeks to help man to face reality with its many problems, and to recognize his own limitations as well as his possibilities for growth. It is dedicated to the development of mature individuals who are capable of living in freedom and of voluntarily restricting their freedom for the larger good of all. It is based on the premise that when man understands himself he can begin to be the master of his own life, rather than the puppet either of his own unconscious drives or of a tyrant with a perverted lust for power.

However, in the course of nearly every man's development, he passes temporarily through a stage of greater susceptibility to totalitarianism. This usually occurs during adolescence, when the youngster becomes aware of his own identity and personality —the authority within himself. To escape the responsibility for being a self he may look for a strong leader outside the home. At an earlier age, in infancy, the more unconscious patterns of compulsion and automatic obedience are laid. With his new sense of selfhood, the youth begins to oppose the adult authorities who previously directed his life.

Becoming conscious of the entity we call ego or self or "I" is a painful mental process. It is not a matter of chance that the feeling of endless longing, of Weltschmerz, is traditionally connected with adolescence. The process of becoming an autonomous and self-growing individual (what one may call one's true self) involves separation from the security of the family. To achieve "internal democracy" the adolescent must separate himself from his protective guiding environment. In so doing he is more than merely intoxicated with his sense of growth and emancipation; his need is to go beyond the ancient rules. Also he is filled with a sense of fear and loneliness. As he enters this new world in which he must assume mature responsibility for his actions, he may become an easy prey for totalitarian propaganda. A personal grudge against growing up may lead him to foresake the struggle for personal maturity.

This problem is particularly acute in Western society not only because of the real ideological-political battle we have to face, but also because of our methods of raising children. So-called primitive groups impose some measure of social responsibility and participation upon the child early in life, and increase it gradually. Our middle-class culture, with its veneration for technology and automation, segregates the child completely in the world of nursery and schoolroom, and then plunges him into adulthood to sink or swim. At this point, many young people shrink from such a test of independence. Many do not want a freedom that carries with it so many burdens and so much loneliness All too many people don't know how to participate in their community life and do not understand the value of their personal vote They are willing to hand back their active freedom in return for continued parental protection, or they may be willing to surrender the idea of government for and by the people to political or economic ideologies which are in fact substitutes for parental images.

Clinically this is also important because many addicts and alcoholics lack the inner freedom and the ego-strength to say "no" to their seducers—social seducers from outside or the tyrants of inner compulsion.

Youth's surrender of individuality is, alas, no guarantee against loneliness and fear. *The real outside world is in no way altered by one's inner choice.* Therefore, the young person who relinquishes his freedom to new parent figures or a new compulsion to conformity develops a curious, dual feeling of love and hate towards all authority. As a result docility and rebellion, submission and hate, live side by side within him. Sometimes he bows completely to authority or tyranny; at other times, often unpredictably, everything in him revolts against his chosen leader. This duality is endless, for one side of his nature continually seeks to overstep the limits which his other, submissive side has imposed. The man who fails to achieve freedom of action knows only two extremes: unquestioning submission and impulsive rebellion. At this stage, the concept of freedom of feeling and thinking is still dormant.

Conversely, the individual who is strong enough to embrace mature adulthood enters into a new kind of freedom. True, this freedom is ambiguous, since it involves the responsibility of making new decisions and confronting new uncertainties. The frontiers of such freedom of action are anarchy and caprice on the one side, and regimentation and suffocation by rules on the other. A compulsive education in the nursery causes in general too much awe for order and regulation. Our technical age coerces nearly everybody into an exaggerated esteem for bureaucracy, institutions, regulations and technical knobs. Sometimes chaos can be a more productive and creative form of order; the less understanding there is of technical know-how, the less magic, awe, anxiety and mental submission will result.

If only we could find an easy formula for the mature attitude towards life! Even if we call it the free democratic spirit, we can still explain more easily what democracy is not than what it is. We can say that our individualizing democracy is the enemy of blind authority. If we wish a more detailed, psychological explanation, we must again contrast it with totalitarianism.

Democracy is against the total regimentation and equalization of its individuals. Democratic freedom still is a great idea full of the inner ambiguities and nostalgias inherent in human ideal. Democratic freedom does not ask for homogeneous integration and smooth social adjustment. Instead, democracy implies a confidence in spontaneity and individual growth. It brings the individual man back into focus as a unique part of the "demos." It is able to postulate progress and the correction of evil. It guards the community against human error without resorting to intimidation. Democracy provides redress for its own errors; totalitarianism considers itself infallible. Whereas totalitarianism controls by whim and is directed by a manipulated public opinion, democracy undertakes to regulate society by law, to respect human nature and to guard its citizens against the tyranny of individuals and organized pressure groups on the one hand and against a power-crazy majority on the other.

Democracy always fights a dual battle. On the one hand, it must limit the resurgence of asocial inner impulses; on the other, it must guard the individual against external forces and ideologies hostile to the democratic way of life.

The inner harmony between social adaptation and self-assertion has to be re-formed in every new environment. Each individual has to fight over and over again the same subtle battle that started during infancy and babyhood. The ego, the self, forms itself through confrontation with reality. Compliance battles with originality, dependence with independence, outer discipline with inner backbone and morale. No culture can escape this inner human battle, though there is a difference in emphasis in every family and in every culture and society.

The battle on two fronts

The combination of internal and external struggle, of a mental conflict on two fronts, renders the Western ideal of an individualized democracy highly vulnerable, particularly when its adherents are unaware of this inherent contradiction. Democracy, by its very nature, will always have to fight against dictatorship from without and destructiveness and laziness from within. Democratic freedom must battle against the individual's inner will to power and also his inner urge to submit. It must battle, too, against the contagious drive for power intruding from over the frontiers and so often backed up by armies.

The inherent inner contrast and ambivalence involved in democratic freedom are particularly well expressed in certain neurotic conflicts. Some persons struggling against environmental pressure want strongly to distinguish themselves and to rise above the crowd. At the same time they long for affirmation and conformity with the group. People want to belong to a mental hierarchy and at the same time want to oppose it. Often they find a temporary solution of their tensions in mutual admiration clubs characterized by strict inner cohesion and hostility toward the outside. Mass opinion is experienced as a deflation of personal opinion, yet there is also a wish for flattering acknowledgment from a majority—a multitude of votes. The search for votes and publicity often connotes an idle approval of self-doubt. A belief in collective superiority covers up lack of self-confidence.

The freedom for one to speak and shout always implies the compulsion for the other to listen.

The freedom towards which democracy strives is not the romantic freedom of adolescent dreams—the negative freedom of being without any restraint—but one of mature stature. Democracy insists on the sacrifices necessary to maintain freedom. It tries to combat the fears that attack men when they are faced with apparently unlimited freedom which can, after all, be misused to satisfy mere instinctual drives.

Because it does not exploit man by myth, primitive magic, mass hypnotism or other psychological means of seduction, democracy is less fascinating for the immature individual than is dictatorial control. Democracy, when it is not involved in a dramatic struggle for survival, may appear uninspiring and drab. It simply demands that men think and judge for themselves; that each individual exercise his full conscious ability in adapting to a changing world; and that genuine public opinion mold the laws that govern the community.

Essentially, democracy means the right to develop one's self rather than to be developed by others. Yet this right, like every other, has to be balanced by a duty. The right to develop the self is impossible without the duty of giving one's energy and attention to the development of others. Democracy is rooted not only in the personal *rights* of the common man but even more in the personal *interests* and *responsibilities* of the common man. When he loses this interest in politics and government, he helps to pave the road to despotism. Democracy demands mental activity of a rather high level from the common man. In our new era of mass communication, that which goes on in the mind of the general public it just as important as the cerebrations of the expert. While the expert may formulate ideas beyond common apprehension, what matters and influences the world is that Tom, Dick and Harry understand the basic content. Official formulations and logical conclusions can kill living thoughts so easily, and smother individual thinking in a barrage of words.

The mystery of freedom is that great inner love men have for it! Those who have tasted real freedom will not waver. Such men have to revolt against unfair pressure. While the pressure accumulates they revolt silently, but at some critical moment the revolt explodes. For those who have experienced the necessity of such outbursts, freedom is life itself! People have learned this in the days of persecution and occupation, in the underground, in the camps, under the threat of demagoguery. We even discover such rebellion in totalitarian countries where, despite the repression and terror, the resistance goes on. Listen, especially, to the jokes circulating around totalitarian regimes. That is the hidden way rebellion is expressed.

Freedom and respect for the individual are rooted in the Old Testament of the Occident, which convinced man that he should make and be responsible for his own history. Such freedom implies that a man can throw off inertia, refuse to cling arbitrarily to tradition, strive for knowledge and accept moral responsibility. Man's fear of freedom is the fear of assuming responsibility.

Yet freedom can be merely an emotional word appealing to infantile conflicts and frustrations experienced by everyone. It can be used as a catchword to spread the suggestion of un-freedom to those who inwardly don't want to be free. It burdens them with new desires and a feeling of rebellion, while in reality some only want to have the freedom to sleep and retreat. What for one group is the freedom to act and create is, for the other, the freedom to give in; and, for a third group, the freedom to rebel and face conflicts. Freedom is dependent on our goals in life and our goals depend on our urge to perfect ourselves. For the man from the Orient it may mean the freedom from physical desires; for Occidental man it is the freedom to fulfill his desires. Our Western freedom of leisure time is derived from *licere*—literally meaning "being permitted *not* to be occupied; not to be engaged in duties."

Again, there is a negative freedom: not being used as an object of interference. And there is a positive freedom, dependent on self-confidence and self-mastery, the active will and self-determination to master oneself.

Freedom can never be completely safeguarded by rules and laws. It is as much dependent on the courage, integrity and responsibility of each individual as it is dependent on these qualities in those who govern us. Every trait in us and our leaders which points to passive submission to power is a betrayal of democratic freedom.

In our American system of democratic government, based on government by consent, three different branches serve to check each other: the executive, the legislative and the judiciary. Yet when there is no will to prevent encroachment and arbitrariness of one by any of the others, this system of mutual checks, too, can degenerate.

Like adolescents who try to hide behind parental authority rather than face mature adulthood, the individual members of a democratic state may tend to shrink from the mental activity and alertness it imposes. They long to take flight into a condition of thoughtless security. Often they would prefer the government or some individual personification of the state—an institution—to solve their problems. It is such desire and inner apathy that breeds totalitarians and conformists. Like an infant the conformist can sleep quietly and transfer all his worries to "Father State." When the intellectuals—that is to say those who pretend to understand—lose their self-control and courage and are possessed only by fears and emotions, the power of prejudice and stupidity gains.

Since within each man lie the seeds of both democracy and totalitarianism, the struggle between the democratic and the totalitarian attitude is fought repeatedly in each individual's lifetime. A man's view of himself and of his fellow men will determine his political creed. Opposing and at the same time coexisting with his wish for liberty and maturity are destructiveness, hate, the desire for power, resistance to independence, and the wish to retreat into irresponsible childhood.

Democracy appeals only to the adult side of man; fascism and totalitarianism tempt his infantile desires.

Totalitarianism is based on a narrow view of mankind. It denies the complexity of the individual, and the struggle between his conscious and unconscious motivations. It denies doubt, ambivalence and contradiction of feelings. It simplifies man, making him into a servile machine that can be put to work by decree. Above all, totalitarianism believes in man as a manipulated "thing," to be directed by the will of the infallible state.

In every psychotherapeutic treatment there comes the moment when the patient has to decide whether or not he will grow up. The knowledge and insight he has gained have to be translated into action. By this time he knows more about himself; his life has at last become an open book. Although he understands himself better, he finds it difficult to leave the dreamland of childhood, with its fantasies, hero-worship and happy endings. But, fortified with a deeper understanding of his inner motivation, he steps out into the world of self-chosen responsibility and limited freedom. Because his image of the world is no longer distorted by immature longings, he is now able to function in it as a mature adult.

Training for democratic freedom

Systematic education towards freedom is possible. Freedom grows as the control over destructive inner drives becomes internalized, and independent of parental and authoritative control.

The building up of our personality and our conscience—ego and super-ego—cannot mature in an enforced and compulsive way. Tyrannical rules can never exist without the supervising iron hand. We must develop the personality through free acceptance or rejection of existing moral values until the inner moral person in people is so strong that they are able to go beyond existing values and stand on their own feet and moral grounds. The choice in favor of freedom lies between self-chosen limitation—the liberation from inner chaos—and the pseudo-freedom of unconscious instinctual chaos. To many people, freedom is an emotional concept of letting themselves go, which really means a dictatorship by dark, instinctual drives. But there is also an intellectual concept of freedom, meaning limiting man's bondage and un-freedom.

Psychological freedom is the freedom of the verifying inner moral person in us. But freedom is far from an unequivocal blessing when we are not ripe for it. There is risk in freedom unless we are able to keep our inner destructiveness under control. One of the most paradoxical struggles we must wage is the struggle against the totalitarian attitude in ourselves.

In order to become free, however, certain outside conditions must be prevented from hampering this moral development of self-control. We have to become increasingly aware of the internal dangers and ills of democracy; laxity, lack of discipline, laziness and unawareness. People have to be aware, for instance, of the tendency of technology to automatize their minds. They have to become aware of the fact that mass media and modern communication are able to bypass people's critical barriers and imprint all kinds of unwanted suggestions on man's brains. They have to know that education can turn us either into weak, uncritical fact-factories or strong personalities. A free democracy has to fight against "mediocrity" in order not to be smothered by mere numbers of automatic votes. Democratic freedom requires from the members of society a highly intelligent appraisal and understanding of the democratic system itself. This very fact makes it rather difficult to advertise or "promote" such a political system. Furthermore, inculcating democracy is just as dangerous as inculcating totalitarianism. It is the essence of democracy that it must be self-chosen; it cannot be imposed.

The paradox of freedom and liberty

Freedom and social planning present no essential contrasts. In order to let freedom grow, we have to plan our controls over the forces that limit freedom. First, there has to be guidance and discipline to develop a strong inner nucleus with which to face the un-freedom of the world. Beyond this, however, people must have the passion and the inner freedom to prosecute those who abuse freedom. They must possess the vitality to attack those who commit mental suicide, dragging down other persons in their wake of passive surrender. Suicidal submission is a kind of "subversion" from within; it is passive surrender to a mechanized world without vital personalities; it is the denial of the personality. There exists in our world too much urge for security and certainty. Such a goal finally leads to death and mental surrender, to automation and the mere existence of the computed man, because life in itself presumes an acceptance of uncertainty. People must have the fervor to stand firmly for freedom of the individual, and for mutual tolerance and dignity, and they must learn not to tolerate the destruction of these values. They must not tolerate those who make use of the glamor of worthy ideas and values—such as freedom and liberty—only to destroy these as soon as they themselves are in power. We must be intolerant of these abuses as long as the battle of mental life versus death of the free-existing personality goes on.

It cannot be emphasized too strongly that liberty is only possible with a strong set of beliefs and moral standards. Man must adhere to self-restrictive rules—moral rules—in order to keep his freedom. When there is a lack of such internal checks, owing to lack of education or to wrong, stereotyped education, then external pressure or even tyranny becomes necessary to check unsocial drives. Then freedom becomes the victim of man's inability to live in freedom and self-control.

Mankind should be guaranteed the right *not* to hear and not to conform, and the more subtle right to defend himself against psychological encroachment and against intervention in the form of oppressive mass propaganda, totalitarian pressure and mental coercion. No compromise or appeasement is possible in dealing with such attitudes. However, we have to watch carefully lest our own mistakes in attacking personal freedom become grist for the totalitarian's mill. Even our denunciations may have a paradoxical effect. Fear and hysteria further totalitarianism. What we need is careful analysis and understanding of such soul-disturbing phenomena. Democracy is the regime fostering the dignity and decency of man and his right to think for himself; the right to have his own opinions and, even more than that, the right *to assert* his own opinion and to protect himself against mental invasion and coercion.

Here we touch a crucial point related to the technique of governing people. There exists, for instance, an intimate relationship between over-centralization of government, bureaucratization, mass participation and totalitarianism.

Mass participation in government, without adequate decentralization that emphasizes the value of variation and individuality and without the possibility of sound selection of leaders, facilitates the creation of the dictatorial leader. The masses then transfer their desire for power to him. The slave participates in a magic way in the glory of the master.

Democratic self-government is determined by restraint and self-limitations, by sportsmanship and fairness, by voluntary observance of the rules of society and by co-operation. These qualities come through disciplined training. In a democratic government, those who have been elected to responsible positions request controls and limitations against themselves, against the inner fraudulence presumptive in every person knowing that no man is without fault. Democracy is not a fight for independence but a mutually regulated interdependence in the service of surplus freedom. Democracy means checking man's tendency to gather unlimited power unto and for himself. It means checking faults in each of us. It minimizes the consequences of man's psychological limitations.

Psychology as a guide for democracy

The modern techniques of brainwashing and menticide—those dictatorial perversions of psychology—can bring almost any man into submission and surrender. Many of the victims of political thought control, brainwashing and menticide were once strong men whose minds and wills, however, were systematically broken and degraded. But although the totalitarians can use their knowledge of the mind for vicious and unscrupulous purposes, a democratic society can and must use its knowledge to help man to grow, to guard his freedom and to understand himself. The totalitarian ideal of man is the instrumental manipulation of man in the service of the monolithic state; the democratic ideal is the dignity and ultimate value of man as a unique, individual being.

Psychological knowledge and psychological treatment may in themselves even generate and liberate the democratic attitude, for psychology is essentially the science of obtaining the *juste-milieu*, of free choice within the framework of man's personal and social limitations. Compared with the million-year span of human existence and evolution, civilization is still in its infancy. Despite historical reversals, man continues to grow, and psychology—no matter how imperfect now—will become one of man's most powerful tools in his struggle for freedom and maturity.

The human mind seems to be much more confused and troubled by the problems of a constructive peace than by the problem of preparing for destructive war. Emotional tensions imposed by the cold, psychological war of peacetime seem to arouse more anticipatory fears and confused passions than the destructive explosions of total war.

During the last war, scientists mobilized every weapon at their command to wage war methodically, not only against the enemy's aggressive physical power, but against his morale and mental strength as well. They tried to beat him emotionally by creating distrust in his leaders, and by stimulating general fear and panic. The Nazi Ministry of Propaganda developed the technique of psychological cold war to such perfection that Goebbels nearly succeeded in hypnotizing, paralyzing and blackmailing the world by the fear of a new world war.

Why can man not apply the same psychological tools and techniques toward the building of a stable peace? To put it more precisely: why cannot the nations of the world systematically mobilize the emotional forces in man to wage constructive psychological peacefare?

Before suggesting answers to those questions, it is necessary to explore the intricate relationship between overt aggression and warfare, as opposed to a reasonable control of aggression and peacefare. The one subject cannot be understood without knowledge of the other.

Man's distorted compulsion to fight

Unlike the instinct-guided animals of prey, man is not a real fighter. Nearly all biologists agree on this point. As we said in an earlier discussion of aggression, man is born without either natural defenses or biological weapons. He remains throughout his life an over-dependent, baby animal without saber teeth and piercing nails. Because of this lack of biological defenses, man was forced into the making of artificial tools for self-protection, and building a safe world became the basis of human civilization. As civilization progressed, man had to repress his cannibalistic past, to delay his devouring hostility and cultivate a fantasy of endless hatred. His tools of aggression are his materialized fantasies. There is something artificial about man's fighting; it is not the outcome of an innate biological pattern but of a secondary fantasy about hostility.

However, before primitive man was conscious of the protective value of social relations in a stable peaceful community, he had not only to defend his life against wild animals but also against his "unadjusted neighbors."

The aggressive, hostile man of the twentieth century, with his highly improved destructive fighting tools, is still, unconsciously, the primitive Neanderthaler who is unsure of his neighbors' intentions. Social beliefs and instinctual insecurity continually imprint upon him the suggestion that he must remain alert, fight and make war, to get away from his deep-seated anxieties and suspicions. For instance, in order to mobilize the Germans for war and to make them more hostile and aggressive, Hitler had to convince them of the necessity of defending themselves against alleged "encirclement" and persecution by outside enemies. It is this so-easily-transmitted delusion of persecution, of being treated unfairly, that arouses the most virulent tempers and ferocities in man.

Throughout history, methodical fighting and warfare has been a kind of sport of noblemen and a few leading clans in the various countries. The more natural "science" of living peacefully together under the protection of law and justice in a non-aggressive society came later. The army of educators is still the most poorly paid lot.

It is as if man has been fascinated by the artificial compulsion of fighting. Some inner feeling of being treated unfairly reverberated with the general battle cry. Man has now grown so used to military pomp that he is hardly able to imagine a society without war, without people waiting for retaliation when defeated. Yet, at the acute impact of violence and attack, there is usually an initial tendency to be passive and to identify with the aggressor. Many people surrender inwardly before the battle is fought. This is why so many people inadvertently side with the enemy when they are convinced that he is stronger. To both individual and collectivity, unilateral weakness represents an invitation to either aggressive dominance or submissive surrender. Immature men prefer the temper tantrums of war to a concerted struggle for peace.

Nevertheless, we see constant proof that even in small tribes and communities the so-called "eternal law of war and aggression" can be checked by the law of justice. Justice and peace protected by powerful laws even have a tendency to expand. Man is not a fighter by nature, but certain instinctual trends, social taboos and prejudices force him to become one. Aggression and hostility never breed security because they always provoke the seeds of retaliation.

Hugo Grotius, the seventeenth-century Dutch humanist, was the first to expound the possibility that the illogical behavior of fighting nations could be controlled by law and international morality. He belonged to a minority persecuted for religious reasons, and weaker minorities always tend to advocate justice and law, rather than power and aggression. It is the same legal point of view adopted by the smaller countries of the United Nations. As soon as man becomes aware of the impossibility of fighting victoriously, and especially of the mutual destructiveness of all fighting, he devotes himself to a nobler inner battle, the mental battle for morals, values and principles.

Thus, in successive ages, we find that kings, generals and civilian war-makers have needed to find increasing justification for waging war. The inner battle for moral values was in conflict with outer battles against the enemy. The insight that war is something stupid and unreasonable—an atavism, a miscalculation in our social organization that could be prevented *if* human beings were wiser—kept growing, in opposition to the traditional compulsion and enthusiasm to fight.

Aggressive war-minded leaders today have to deal more and more with an uneasy public opinion. They have to take into account an increasing moral resistance to war. Yet, the moral issue has never been so strong that a reasonable justification could not be found to silence the voice of peace. Nowadays, there is the anticipation and fear of total atomic destruction, leading to panic and renewed fantasies of retaliation. Mankind is stranded in an impasse of paradoxes, a vicious circle of fear and violence and revenge. But man's pessimism is usually a device to disguise his apathy, passivity and other frailties.

The time for active, psychological means of fighting the danger of war and man's self-destructive tendencies is urgent and long past due.

What is psychological warfare?

The systematic influencing of public opinion to make people favor the waging of a future war was practiced over a century ago by Napoleon in his "Bureau de l'opinion publique." The Nazis, however, developed the manipulation of an anguished public spirit into a huge scientific machinery. Their psychological warfare became a new form of the aggressive strategy of persuasion in peacetime, the so-called "war between wars," also called the *phony war* or the *cold war*. As a result of Germany's systematic attack on European morale and its intimidating war of nerves against neighboring countries, other nations began to organize (but too late) their own psychological defenses. It was only in the second half of World War II that they were able to achieve some measure of success.

Psychological warfare has two principle aims: first, to paralyze and confuse the enemy by psychological means—a euphemism for political blackmail; second, to stimulate and galvanize the fighting morale of one's own country by making the people more war-minded than they would normally be. The Nazis were using various psychological threats and intimidations in full peacetime. At the same time the cold war is a battle for the verbal initiative in capturing the world's headlines. Thus psychological warfare grows into a science of mutual provocation and arousal of mutual distrust.

Hitler's weapon of fear and panic paralyzed Europe before a single shot was fired. The French let him reoccupy the Rhineland in 1936. The British chancellor raised his umbrella in vain against Hitler's hypnosis. Austria and Czechoslovakia were the first victims of Hitler's psychological artillery, when he walked in without any shots being fired. Rumor, slander and suspicion were Hitler's most important mental tools of aggression. The Nazis instructed their fifth columnists to spread devastating and paralyzing rumors in neighboring countries, especially in France.

Warfare with words

Used as a tool of terror and mass-hypnosis, fear can have a paralyzing effect on the public. Hitler's method with the German masses was, in his own words, to make "ruthless fanatics out of them." Through the use of a monotonous repetition of lies and half-truths, by the mind-dulling technique of repetitious speeches that people were compelled to listen to, and with the aid of press, radio and films, Hitler "fanaticized" his people into becoming submissive servile fighters.

There is a general belief in the magic of the printed word. Words on newsprint, slogans repeated daily, misunderstood issues—all mesmerize the uncritical masses. Printed words look like absolute truths. Critical people may try to ward off these suggestions, but the massive daily ration of new propagandistic words finally weakens their resistance. In the cold war way of thinking, the propaganda value of a meeting is more important than the problems that might be solved at the meeting.

This is one of the leading dangers and strengths of the press. We can use public information to stir up man's feelings for war and destruction; we can also use it to describe and instill the fundamentals of peace.

Nazi strategists knew that the spoken word heard via the radio or at huge mass meetings could have an even greater contaminative and hypnotizing influence. The German masses were subjected to long, boring speeches and the repetition of monotonous syllables. Political leaders used the narcotizing ecstasy of mystical ideologies and political mythology to force people into an even deeper trance. This imitated the well-known technique of hypnotizing patients by boring, soothing words. The more submissive listening ear is more likely to accept lies than the more critical reading and verifying eye.

People all over the world must learn that speeches about the ideal of peace and genuine peaceful intentions are not necessarily the same.

Remember Hitler's simple tranquilizing technique of promising his people all they wanted. Thus he repeatedly promised peace, socialism, wealth, and full employment to the German people. He always aroused their imagination positively. From time to time he also aroused the romantic and heroic wish to die for the fatherland. But he never spoke directly about depressing subjects, about the risk of his policies, or about the suffering of war. These bad things happened only to the scapegoats. The aim of his propaganda was to make passive followers and fellow megalomaniacs out of the Germans. In the delusion that their vocation was to fight for the Fuehrer's delusions, many of them ultimately perished with him in the war's last holocaust.

Even more aggressive as a psychological means of attack are terrorizing slogans and films. Hitler showed in Oslo the horrible film of the destruction of Warsaw just a few days before the invasion of Norway. Some totalitarians try to use the same technique of softening up their adversaries by confusing and anxiety-provoking incidents. Cynical and satirical radio broadcasts also have a demoralizing effect. At the end of the war, the strategic bombardment of slogans from the Allied psychological services created as much panic among the enemy population as did the real bombardments. Goebbels, who saw the psychological lead slipping out of his hands, had to warn the people ferociously against the many forms of demoralizing rumors floating around Germany, rumors people had picked up from Allied broadcasts.

The psychological influence of some of these new strategic weapons, however, was less penetrating than the Germans had imagined it would be. London, for example, was never thrown into a panic by Hitler's repeated air attacks. Yet the defensive power of France's Maginot line was largely broken through by psychological means which paralyzed the will of the defenders.

It is wise to remember that the psychological weapon does not always succeed entirely—not even the modern attempts at ideological persuasion and thought-control. People accustomed to thinking for themselves—as is the habit in a real democracy—gradually become immune to propaganda and develop a resistance to the most insidious slogans. Even if the major part of the press is in the hands of one of the parties, people in a country where some tradition of freedom is still alive learn to resist the daily suggestive headlines and express their own free opinions. Only dictatorship and its concomitant terror, fear and tension make free private opinion too risky, and prepare the people for final submission.

Are people infected with a suggestion of unavoidable war?

Even though the dictator's psychological weapons do not have that tremendous influence the Nazis and Russian strategists imagined, the danger does exist in the form of a slow-acting contamination with the opinions of the enemy. The result of various aggressive methods used in defense and in waging war is that every fighter unwittingly becomes accustomed to identifying himself with the attacking enemy. In every war, dangerous, mutual identification can be detected which may later cause a new war. When this happens, the principle for which people think they are fighting gets lost in the mutual mental contagion.

In our epoch it is no longer merely a question of overthrowing Nazism or Fascism or combatting totalitarian tyranny. There is a more subtle battle going on to rid ourselves of various unconscious identifications with excited aggressors in the world and to drop authoritarian attitudes which we have unwittingly adopted. The aggressive attitude of wartime remains for years in all of us, as was observed clearly in many postwar neuroses. People may construct various political justifications for their militant attitudes, but what is significant psychologically is that the poisonous suggestion of man as an eternally fighting warrior is kept alive.

Fighting and systematic warfare are unnatural but they remain active because of certain fallacies of group life and neurotic developments within the individual.

Is it possible to turn man's aggressive and war-loving delusions into more human and more civilized channels? Is it possible to stop the paradoxical craziness of violence in the service of truth and justice? Is it possible to create social organizations to make people more susceptible to a mentality of peace? We know that it is possible to wage rather effective psychological warfare, but might we also engage in psychological *peacefare,* a strategy of transferring the illusion of aggressiveness into more valuable social expressions?

What can modern psychology contribute?

Psychology has already been called upon to heal some of the world's confusions, although so far on only a rather small scale. During World War II, psychologists were able to be helpful in dealing with problems relative to vagrant youths, displaced persons, towns in panic and many individual citizens in distress. I am sure that the constructive help of psychologists can be even greater in time of peace.

In London during the war years, I tried—with friends and colleagues of the Inter-Allied Psychological Study Group—to formulate what actual psychology should be able to accomplish. Our conclusions are summed up in these few paragraphs:

1. Psychology can teach people a more general *psychological approach* to problems, that is to say, a *human* approach rather than merely a political one. Psychologists can plead for greater objectivity in emotional circumstances. Psychologists can direct attention to hidden, unconscious human motives. Psychologists are more acquainted than the layman with the ambivalence of human opinions, realizing that people who profess to hate X and Y often hide a deep-seated love for them. Psychologists can show again and again how many so-called logical official arguments actually represent confused emotions. For a practical example of the psychological approach to a wartime problem, I can mention a discussion that came up regarding the advisability of dropping food parcels to starving Allies behind enemy lines. The military view was that the Germans would keep the food, that

this would serve only to help the enemy. The psychologist could show that sending food to the enemy would be a direct attack on enemy morale: "so sure are the Allies of victory that they do not mind sending food." Basically, the dropping of food was a psychological measure, weakening the enemy's confidence while, at the same time, increasing the hope of the starving friends in occupied territory.

2. Psychologists must teach a more *individualizing approach* in relation to the problems of mankind. Behind the faceless "masses" there is always the unique human being with his individual variety of reactions. All decisions and mistakes are ultimately made by individuals and their subjective evaluations. Politicians often forget how much the personal mental state of the leading few contributes to the mental state of the world.

We tried to put this point into practice via our report to UNRRA on how to deal with displaced people. We warned repeatedly against the so-called official "parcel politics." Human beings are not parcel-post packages, they are subjects, not objects. You cannot handle them in a mechanical way, sending them hither and thither. Parcel politics arouses only rebellion and reactive aggression.

3. Psychologists can influence *the methods of political investigation* Politics and social psychology were formerly studied, for the most part, behind the theoretical desk. Modern psychologists plead for a more clinical approach, encouraging on-the-spot studies by trained field workers who are truly objective observers. Political forecasts and impulsive actions could then be analyzed according to motivations of the suggestor and the impact of the suggestion.

At the end of the war, our group was able to organize a meeting to consider the different methods of social investigation and clinical field work in Europe.

4. Psychologists advise the actualization of the conflict. Don't

delay or hide the problem because of its consequences. Where there is a conflict, recognize it immediately, and try to ask the right questions. Every diplomatic and political delay in solving a problem (that is to say, by not touching it because of its complications) increases hidden tensions and aggression and increases the chance of a new aggressive explosion. Don't expect that time itself will bring a happy outcome. Time, as such, does not heal, although, as it passes, new problems may obscure the old ones. Analyze the situation now; call a spade a spade, and let people agree about what they disagree.

5. Repeat a simple intelligent viewpoint, even when your redundance is boring to many people. One adequate piece of advice is usually not enough. Psychologists have to be sure to reach the ears of the public. Therefore, they have to repeat and repeat again.

People can learn to understand that what they believe in is not necessarily their own belief, but something adopted because of emotional pressure. They must be taught that the pessimistic view of reality is just as much a trick of the mind as unjustified optimism. Pessimism usually is a disguise and justification for man's self-pity—a deep, inner defense against a yearning for dependency.

Modern psychological and educational techniques are able to spread intelligent reactions instead of those which are merely emotional. But psychologists, of course, too, must be alert. They must never be allowed to hide behind tiredness and passivity.

Toward psychological peacefare

Analyzing pacifist movements of the past, we see that they frequently did not get at the psychological roots of warfare. Although presumably based on a sweet, idealistic moral code, they actually derived from a deep-seated personal fear of war and aggression. The fears of some of the most fervent pacifists can even be explained as stemming from the peace-seekers' own repressed hostility. Man's guilt feelings about inner hate and hostility can be tremendous and are sometimes alleviated by a mask of meekness and weakness. By promoting a frustrated "soft" pacifist attitude, warmongers are able, quite cynically, to intimidate future enemies. Thus, the Nazis promoted various pacifistic movements in neighboring countries, while in Germany itself pacifists were persecuted. Through this subterfuge they hoped to undermine their neighbors. The best way to subdue your neighbors is to make submissive pacifists of them and then blackmail their need for peace.

Positive peacefare, therefore, will have to encourage not an emotional, escapist attitude toward peace, but a constructive feeling of mental and moral strength. It must be a science of tolerable rivalry; of peaceful co-existence *not* to be used as a breathing spell for renewed coercion. The techniques of constructive peace are much more difficult and subtle than those of destructive war!

Gandhi, in his movement for armorless passive resistance against the British occupiers, always emphasized that one had to be fearless for *satyagraha.* Once you face your enemy with residual fear in your heart or with semi-conviction, you don't disarm him but only arouse more hostility and reprisal instead.

There is another reason why earlier forms of peacefare usually failed. Since men turned by "mistake" into aggressive animals of prey, all the other techniques of living have been more or less dependent on war techniques. Man's need to protect and defend himself in an emergency of war has often shaken him out of his technological apathy and led him to new inventions. The unfortunate result is that man's defensive techniques—his tools and toys of destruction—often seize him in their fascinating grip, as we see in the case of the aftermath of the atomic bomb. The fear of this weapon's tremendous destructive power still keeps the human mind nearly paralyzed. The eerie magic thought of turning the world into Armageddon with one push of the button keeps man's mind on the brink of awe and panic. The only answer people tentatively find is to make more and greater bombs than their potential enemies can make. In the meantime, these new weapons increase anticipatory fears and incite people to make still better explosives, until everyone is caught in a vicious circle not far removed from the destructive megalomania of psychotics.

The former League of Nations represented an attempt at attaining world peace but on a rather theoretical basis. The League was not even a negotiation chamber. It did not take into consideration that power politics is still the triumphant competitor of justice and that modern economics is based more on power and the will to dominate than on righteous division of wealth.

Nevertheless, the world will have to repeat and repeat this international experiment and gradually correct its mistakes. The danger is that one-sided overconfidence in the usefulness of an existing international organization usually connotes some psychological disguise of apathy, passivity, and sabotage. Every human offer and alert activity has to start within oneself.

The United Nations is an improvement over the League because it devotes itself more to the science and practice of possible peace; in other words, to peaceful coexistence of different human powers without attempts at ideological reformation.

Has the United Nations so far created a strong foundation for a constructive peace? I doubt it. International policy is composed to a large extent of cold legal thinking covering up egocentric national issues. Most of the arguments are well-chosen verbal justifications for cold war bargaining rather than real attempts to solve problems.

In peacefare, just as in psychological warfare, we must reach the emotions of human beings, and this means always *individual* human beings. A theoretical, juridical or diplomatic siege at a distant U.N. tower will not help the people; it does not turn distant human bias and aggression into cooperation. Yet, it is only the will to cooperate that counts, and the way a U.N. decision is able (and permitted) to confront the wills and emotions of the individual in a faraway country.

The new strategy of psychological peacefare—the building of collective foundations of peace—may tackle the problem of peace from the following three angles·

(a) Psychological
(b) Juridical
(c) Educational

I will deal with them here very briefly:

(a) On the *psychological* side, the U.N. could concentrate more on reaching the minds of individuals in the member states and nations, rather than only the minds of statesmen and governments who are, for the most part, deeply frozen in biased attitudes. It is a wrong notion that only diplomatic mediation reaches the core of human problems. An international mentality with a feeling of mutual goodwill has to be created in the countries themselves. If the people cannot defrost their intractable representatives, who else can?

This reaching of the minds of individuals can be done by press, radio, books and all the other communicative media for the transmission of knowledge—just as in psychological warfare. Individuals must gradually learn to identify themselves not only with nationalistic ideals, but with those of the new stabilizing international community; in other words, with the great moral issues and images of our time.

The U.N. should establish a more elaborate department of international human relations, where experts (who, during the hot and cold wars, handled their negative psychological weapons so successfully), could use their psychological inventiveness to reach the people individually.

Such a department should also have the task of studying and detecting untamed hostility and aggression wherever it exists in the world. A new science of *political psychology* has to grow. Its objectives are circumspect: to study the psychology of war and peace in individual and collectivity and also the motivations of those political leaders who make war or are driven to declare war. Psychological observation posts could be maintained in various countries to record the sentiments of different people towards the united efforts to maintain peace.

My principal and nearly Utopian point is that the U.N. should have some *token* representation in the various countries. Only then can psychologists begin practical field work in the service of preserving peace.

Will such a representation of the United Nations be allowed to reach individuals directly? Technically the problem would not be too difficult; politically, however, many nations would protest against such intrusion into their "sacred" sovereignty and would try to select and censor the news and suggestions that the United Nations would like to spread.

If, however, a cautious, token attempt at such *two-way representation* and communication were able to succeed—the country sends representatives to the U.N., the U.N. sends representatives to the countries—its psychological influence would gradually grow.

We have to realize that well-directed psychological contact and influence on individuals reaches deeper than any mechanical, political catchword. United Nations representatives dedicated to cultural and psychological activities in the various countries could have a great stabilizing future.

The catchwords "national defense" have to be gradually unmasked. The irony of defense is that it always arouses counter-aggression and counter-armament and "anti-antis," but nothing positive. The actual danger of an equilibrium of powers in peaceful co-existence is that it hides dynamite. Any wrong spark may cause an explosion.

Yet, human aggressiveness and destructiveness can be conquered by cultural and educational means; we know that from experiences with criminals. The usual attempts at sublimating man's hostility by games and sports unfortunately tend to degenerate into unsportsmanlike aggression and suggest even at Olympiades the competitive fight for personal ambition and pride.

Fair play, however, and the sublimation of aggression into physical and cultural contests can be made again the purpose of sport if international contests and Olympiades could be made part of a positive U.N. program.

Children could begin to experience these fairer evaluations in their own school communities. Educating children to play a fair sportsmanlike game teaches them to check their atavistic aggressive qualities, especially when they are taught to think about them and deliberate at the same time. The feeling of fairness and justice is less spoiled at the school age.

Indeed, man's aggressiveness and primitive craving for power and destruction can be transformed. His suicidal and mass-suicidal tendencies can be cured. The transformation of this unchecked energy into productive labor is one of the greatest incentives to creation and creativity. There is a psychological connection between unemployment, a failing economy, increased mutual aggressiveness and lack of creative incentives. Happily enough, the United Nations and its members realize already that attempts at international collaboration will fail unless there is general gainful employment and an implicit opportunity for challenge and creativeness for people throughout the world.

A difficult but intricate problem of psychological peacefare is that of *mental contagion*. It is, alas, much easier to regress a crowd towards animal behavior than to transmit habits of self-restraint. Fascism, tyranny and power politics have a tendency to spread their influence like infectious diseases to other countries. Man easily falls back into his archaic delusion of being an omnipotent magician and warrior and animal of prey. Modern techniques of communication make it nearly impossible to stop such aggressive contagion and mental pressure at a frontier.

Aggressiveness, bellicosity and dictatorial attitudes and feelings are easily transplanted from one authoritarian center to another country.

Freedom and civilization can also be infectious—even democratic dignity—but they work more slowly. A future international organization must somehow try to lay down rules to break up sources of poisonous political contamination.

(b) On the *juridical* and *legal* side, psychologists and social scientists should study more carefully than heretofore the tenets and principles of justice. The old League of Nations was ruled by theoretical treaties and a rather archaic disguising diplomacy. The League had no nimbus of morality, no moral voice, no common code of ethics designed for the people's benefit. The idea of justice for all is now tentatively adopted in the U.N.'s International Charter of Human Rights, but has not permeated to the general public, nor do the people in various nations realize that some of the juridical treaties were drawn for their benefit. Nevertheless, the average individual has a rather good practical feeling for justice and injustice, as we see in studies of persecuted minorities. The weaker, persecuted party is well aware that autonomous rules must be sacrificed for the sake of justice and communal law. The stronger party hates to give up its private power and "sacred" sovereignty in the service of higher justice.

The core of the juridical question is the giving up of sovereign authority. For instance, the question of a real disarmament cannot be solved without effective mutual inspection.

In the long run, individuals must have the nobility to ask their own states and nations to sacrifice national privileges for the sake of a more stable international community based on law and justice. They must proceed in the same way as they did when they surrendered part of their privacy and autonomy to their own governments in the service of legalized and codified collaboration.

This, however, will only be possible after a preliminary co-operation between the big powers has been established.

The International Charter of Human Rights gives certain basic guarantees of freedom and justice to all individuals and minorities in the world. The existing Charter, if it could be made a more active principle, would not immediately prevent injustice, but it would constitute the first small symbolic and legal *sacrifice* of each state's national pride for the sake of universal human rights. The various executives will gradually have to follow where the convictions in the hearts of the nations point the way. In the meantime, the Charter can stimulate—if publicized and discussed—new identifications with an international legal code and a world community.

New courts of justice—sponsored by the U.N.—will have to be set up in order to carry out the international charter. There cannot merely be one court for settling big problems; we will need several courts of international character in different countries to serve as token watchdogs for the fundamental rights of the individual. Such courts would have more of a *psychological* than a juridical function. In the beginning, they would be bombarded with all sorts of querulous complaints and appeals, but in the end they would serve as ambassadors of the international idea of justice and lawful society. When functioning more smoothly they would form the best defense possible against the fear and anxiety that unlimited national power arouses.

(c) On the *educational* side, every child can be imbued with constructive feelings toward peace and internationalism. The child understands the golden rule: do unto others as you would have them do unto you. Here is where a subtle psychological task of UNESCO begins. Let us not forget that youth, above all, has been influenced by pugnacity and war. Children are impregnated daily with the propagandistic delusion that man is an eternal warrior. For many youngsters, there still is little or no moral directive from the world of parents or older people, so they create their own gangs with strict "legal" rules.

Minimum standards of education will have to be established. But let us not forget that it is especially the spirit of education that counts. Will we train children again and again for the "soldatesque" idea of destruction or will we educate them for freedom and responsibility?

Those who put all their hopes in a greater development of mechanical science and technology deny the psychological fact that technology unobtrusively is a champion of passivity, easiness and luxury. It teaches people that the shortest way is the best way, while psychology tells us that man needs just the opposite—challenge and resistance—in order to become a personality. Technology delivers machines of destruction as well as machines for greater production. But no machine teaches us empathy, compassion and reverence—the qualities we need so very much for peace.

Technology creates the delusion of a magic fulfillment of material yearnings, making us fat, complacent and torpid. The dire need to build up good human relations and mutual tolerance is replaced by the fascinating pushbuttons of the automaton.

The most dangerous thing in the world is the mixture of technological know-how with undisciplined passions.

There exists a wrong idea of hero-worship in the world. Because man lives in so much fear and insecurity, he wants to be encouraged by the artificial image of the brave warrior and hero. The image of a pugnacious hero of peace like Gandhi has to be better developed. History lessons put too much stress on warfare. More attention should be paid to man's cultural development. Foreign languages and civilizations will have to be taught more extensively, and student exchange with foreign universities facilitated even more than at the present time. All education is, in essence, education for civilization—not Eastern civilization nor Western civilization, but common civilization. This means that we must stimulate man's participation in civil and cultural life, and breed respect for man's intellect and capacity for understanding. We must make young people enthusiastic again for the great ideas, and inspire them to struggle not only with machinery and gadgets but with thoughts.

In addition to these specific scholastic subjects, entirely new fields of education must be opened. Active education for liberty and social responsibility must be an essential part of the school education. The school should more clearly represent real society with its courts and parliaments and institutions. These institutions, in play form, can be set up at the schools in order to let the youngster practice the acceptance of challenge and tolerance. We must teach youngsters to combat our ideas in order to inspire them with our ideas. We will have to encourage new educational endeavors that embody the study of international civics and politics, of simple social science and elementary characterology

Man must learn to conceive and to master his own history. Modern education is able to rear children with a positive sense for tolerance towards unknown human beings, and with respect for justice. Prejudice is something artificial and can easily be understood as caused by social suggestions. Prejudice starts in the family and the classroom. Experiments in grade schools have proved that children are interested in dealing with social and legal conflicts and especially in knowledge about their differences in character. This interest in each other may become the beginning of better self-knowledge. Pacificism and internationalism, too, start in the family and in the classroom. The concept of international justice starts with the game of justice and mutual tolerance in classroom and youth club.

I have attempted here only a brief exploration of the subject of psychological peacefare—the forgotten science that requires both wisdom and vision. Because of man's atavistic aggressiveness, and the destructive suggestions around him, there is enormous resistance against the strategy of peacefare. Yet, this is the science of honestly acknowledging human mistakes instead of turning them into boastful braveries. People dare not hope; dare not believe in their own constructive sense. Because of the fear and suspicion in the world, many people surrender passively to the idea of misery and fate. They even find it boring to use their brains and to discuss the positive means of peace and cooperation.

How much brain power has been directed toward the development of psychological warfare and other artificial aggressive tools of war! We must now learn to use even more brain power to forge the fundamental means of peace. Again, peace begins in the formation of human tolerance, in the family and in the classroom.

The new challenge to mankind is to rid ourselves of atavistic, pugnacious delusions and to construct what civilization really can be. People are much too susceptible to the anticipation of threatening war. However, if the human mind is able to indulge in war—an unnatural social habit formation—it must be even better able to bar war.

That is the challenge of the new science of psychological peacefare.

CHAPTER SEVEN

That Difficult Peace of Mind

Usually we preach when we want others to believe what we don't quite believe ourselves. We can preach about God and the last things of the world, or we can preach about nothingness, picturing the universe as a flimsy trifle. A great danger of our technical age is modern man's temptation to retreat into this woeful delight in nothingness with its hidden wake of subjective grandeur . . . and loneliness. Seeking an empty peace of mind, he can withdraw into artificial ecstasy, escaping reality via alcoholic oblivion, the delight of tranquilizers, or through the passive distractions of TV screen, card games or cabaret.

Even scientific specialism can be a form of retreat from the simple problems of the world. Here the escape mechanisms are the pedantic self-deceit of clichés and word fetishism, a conforming ritualistic attitude of scientific formulations. For an example, I cannot do better than describe an experience from my own practice.

The voice of the woman on the couch was appealing and

earnest. "Doctor, how can you close your eyes at night and sleep quietly when all the dark problems of our world are mounting on you? Will we survive? Will our children survive?"

I waited a moment and asked a question in return. "How many hours do *you* think and work to solve these problems?"

At this, the patient grew silent, and seemed annoyed. She was restless, and didn't speak for a long time. "A good point," she said finally. "But it is you, in the first place, who should be burdened with these nerve-wracking problems of our time."

Now it was my turn to be silent. What the patient had said was true and not true at the same time. She had presented an objective judgment of the epoch, but I knew that she had also communicated something deeply hidden about herself.

We had been entangled in a long, subtle struggle for human contact. She was an older colleague, well-known professionally, who had asked me for help about her personal despair. I had been flabbergasted. I knew her publications. logically condensed surveys of the literature of our common profession. I had heard her lectures and shared the official esteem for her clear erudition.

Yet her subjective picture was so completely different from what the world knew about her. The woman knew all the psychiatric books—even pages and quotations—but she had never learned to make human contact with her fellow beings. In her practice she had failed, or at least firmly believed she had failed.

In the beginning I felt hesitant about treating her; we don't like to treat our teachers. As she gradually unfolded her life history, I saw a life so bare of any affection that I could understand why she had taken refuge in a system of intellectual knowledge with no trace of emotional involvement or intuitive apprehension. Now, even in her refuge, she had periods of growing despair which had gradually brought her to treatment by a colleague.

The only child of well-to-do older parents, both scientists, she had been educated in a scientific system of do's and don'ts. She remembered that at a very young age she had been able to follow her parents' scientific discussions; there was no memory at all of ever being cuddled or kissed. Later in treatment, memories came up of periods of great depression in her early childhood when she was alone at home and nobody played with her. Happily enough she had been able to use her good intellect as an instrument for repressing her feelings. She had become over-argumentative toward her parents, and a voracious reader. Books were her only friends. Outside the family she was a withdrawn, shy girl excelling in her intellectual gifts. She had begun her study of psychiatry out of a vague feeling that this would help her, but her intellectualism had entangled her more and more in the facts. She was never able to let a man caress or kiss her, and never had had any sexual experience. She lived in a self-chosen prison of bookish knowledge, afraid to confess to anyone her utter loneliness.

Now she was making a last attempt to reach a world of human inter-communication that she had never been able to enter.

Describing the course of her treatment is not my purpose here. Although her loneliness could not be completely conquered, she was able to become a good child guidance counselor.

My reason for citing this experience is to reveal what it taught *me.* At first I became gradually dragged into her despair. Who could repay to this older woman what the world (her parents) had withheld from her? At that time I was not so aware of the function of self-damaging principles and injustice-collecting in the patient herself. She used isolation and retreat to punish her imaginary enemies. But we both could meet on the subject of what a tricky instrument man's intellect can be. She had developed a rather cynical objectivity toward her own profession and was an active member of the "paper delivery mill," in which authors quote each other mutually while repressing the problems they don't dare to touch. Scientific conformity and quotation-mania easily lead to lack of self-respect.

Her moments of despair were her true moments of reality. Feeling all the woes of the world, she felt at least a living being.

"But, Doctor, how can you close your eyes at night and sleep quietly when all the dark problems of our world are mounting on you?" Now I knew that she was talking about her unsolved problems of the heart.

Her problem was her intellectualization; her denial of emotions, her denial of her yearning for warmth and contact. True, she was a lonely creature. She had experienced the loneliness of not being able to communicate and break the shell of her isolation. Behind her intellectual front of clarity and know-it-allness, however, was the fear of her inner terror and hostility—the formerly justified hostility she had felt toward her parents. She was repeating her old game of hide-and-seek all over again. She needed her patients and colleagues in order to exist as a being herself, but at the same time she hated them.

As a result of treating her, I asked myself several times: Do I myself compulsively need to treat patients to keep my own peace of mind? Do I myself live in an ivory tower, even though I have better contact and rapport than my esteemed colleague? The answers to those questions were often difficult to give.

It is a peculiar trick of the mind to make problems complicated when they can be said-and-done in a simple way. I remember how I became rigidly scientific and over-intelligent in my analysis whenever I wanted to evade the simple consequences of action. The search for pseudo-profoundness is the simple trick of an unwilling heart.

My patient helped me recognize this when she talked about confusion and asked questions under the guise of hoping to understand me better. It was the same old trick of sophistication in order to escape simple moral actions.

Sometimes it is a fear of clarity that pushes us into unchecked violence. Sometimes we make more mysterious what can be solved with a kind deed. Scientific sophistication and labelization can truly protect us against clarity.

My patient presented me with repeated examples of her false adoration of the obscure, the incomprehensible and the confused. She demonstrated her love of cynicism and her ruthless mechanical handling of other people's lives, all because somehow she could not accept a loving responsibility. Because of her disinterest in others, she was never a part of the world until her treatment had impact.

The art of understanding, of empathy and comprehension is not dependent on professional training. No diploma covers intuition and the shaping of original ideas. Gradually my patient became less severe and cynical with her own patients and more tolerant to colleagues even when they knew less than she did. In time, her hostile over-sophistication changed to a growing interest in the hidden child in herself and eventually in all those other children who feel lost in a cold, mechanical world. Her later decision toward a child guidance practice was the final outcome of this inner change.

In work with children especially, the therapist learns to realize that he always can do something. In the subtle equilibrium of childhood, the process of growth—for better or for worse—can be guided with greater success than in adults. In the treatment of children one realizes that cure is always possible. Even the rebellious so-called "criminality" in children is our great hope for the future. It is educational boredom that leads young people to misdeeds. Great care must be taken, of course, not to replace common sense and sympathy with mere scientific sophistication, offering the child tests and quizzes instead of a guiding hand. I once saw a school girl in panic, after her first affair, because of this sort of treatment. She had wanted desperately to speak intimately with a guidance counselor but, instead, spent weeks going through the mill of a battery of tests.

Nobody is an island, yet everybody is. All creative action occurs in utter loneliness. It is that magic soliloquy with oneself that takes shape in words and music and form. Such creativity is the loneliness of man's uniqueness. It creates the fear of being hurt and humiliated.

Yet the little child in us, so dependent on intimacy and togetherness, may feel sorry for himself and transform his true human activity into a feeling of utter deprivation and loss. Self-pity may eventually become a substitute joy and the breeding of deprivation and bitterness, a goal. In a world that burdens a child too heavily with cold anxiety without human ties, suicidal destructiveness easily develops as a devious means to punish imaginary enemies.

I have called war a primitive form of expressing aggression and hostility. This is a trite generalization, and, like all generalizations, only partially true. There are other bitter battlefronts in the world: economic, social, intellectual, psychological and spiritual. Often the soul is more cruelly hurt by insidious propaganda than the body is wounded by bullets or shell fragments. Many fall victim to false insinuations and accusations, but in a true democracy man is trained to take these psychological blows on the chin. The psychology of peace includes man's willingness to tolerate injustice temporarily and to suffer personal defeat without self-pity. Life consists not only of fighting for justice but also of being able to temporarily bear injustice. An animal is inclined to react violently when it is hit, but man can learn to withdraw and think wisely before acting, provided he doesn't enclose himself in his tower of intellect. Such imprisoned scholars come easily into a rage again. Man can learn *not* to repeat his mistakes. Between the hostile stimulus from outside and the human reaction to it from within, the human *idea* takes shape and thinking is freedom. But thinking is only freedom when it is creative and original; not when it is done automatically.

To be free is typically human. It means a gradual deliverance from uncontrolled instinctual action. An animal is bound to live according to an innate, instinctual plan and, in some cases, man also lives like such an automaton. But if he is not tied inextricably to the primitive beast within him, he has other alternatives —all the possibilities furnished by reason. A guiding idea releases man from the bondage of his unchecked instincts.

Peace is an idea; war a discharge. Peace calls for careful consideration and wisdom; war demands recklessness and brute power. Totalitarianism is systematized human aggression and need for power. It reigns like the rigid pecking order among animals: I am stronger so you are my slave. Totalitarian "peace" is a semantic decoy for submission.

Aggressive totalitarianism in the world cannot be conquered until inner despotism in the individual has been conquered Aggression from without cannot be overcome until we learn to deal with our aggressiveness from within. But this inner aggression cannot be conquered unless fear and frustration are conquered first. Behind our confused attitudes today there is a great fear, a fear which seeks protection behind defensive atomic strategy and panicky expectations of the world's doom. In the meantime we forget to build up the more positive forces of a constructive peace.

From my own profession I have learned how very difficult the inner battle is against snobbish feelings, those tenacious feelings of grandeur that all people cherish more or less as a remainder of man's magic thinking from early childhood. It is one of the greatest obstacles blocking human relationships. It keeps us away from groups because we think they are not cultural enough or not racially pure enough. It is this infantile feeling that whispers to us that other people are boring, don't know as much as we know or don't offer interesting conversation. It impels us to run away from silence and relaxed encounter with our fellow beings, because we are constantly measuring them, without having value and capacity ourselves. In the midst of this continual measuring, we become indifferent towards the fate of others since they have become only a source for judgment, not affectionate relationships.

This measuring snobbishness can be detected even in the circle of psychologists. Many look at themselves as adepts initiated into mysterious knowledge and secret nomenclature that gives them the right to look down on other therapists.

In some phases of self-investigation, I myself had to struggle with this childish evil much more than I was aware Psychiatric experience teaches us that everybody is important: the weak-minded and the genius; the weak-hearted and the hero; the passive escapist and the criminal. It teaches us too that nobody becomes a therapist—or a politician or a tyrant—without his subjective motivations.

Snobbish rejection of the so-called poorer in culture and civilization reflects, for the most part, something lacking in oneself. It means denial of one's own childhood; denial of the common stupidities we all go through. Those who excuse themselves and retreat to ivory towers reduce their capacity to love and weaken their human ties, because we all live in the lives of others as they live in ours. What we usually reject as stupid, or inferior, or impure, represents what we secretly reject in ourselves. We are afraid to acknowledge those reflections of our own limitations. Others, acting as mirrors, make us afraid and this is why we want to destroy them.

What I saw so clearly as a youngster—that the future would belong to psychology and anthropology—still repeats itself in my mind. True, I have learned since then that such Utopian expectations were conditioned by sad circumstances in my own life. But I learned to be a Utopian. People need action for the sake of a goal even when error and failure threaten. These are the proud words of Holland's liberator, William the Silent: "We do not need hope in order to persevere, neither success in order to continue; faith is enough."

I *had to* believe in our age of psychology in order to keep myself going straight under the pressure of the circumstances. Even so, I became aware of the dangers of knowledge and scientific insight. It all depends on who will use this reservoir of knowledge and what his motives for application are. All knowledge can be used for right *or* wrong. The final test for the value of knowledge is a matter of the heart. Too much specialization can separate brain from heart and intellect from emotion. Our world must fight with an open visor against world-wide fear and human destructiveness. Oppression in the world breeds hatred and revenge. Ideals cannot easily be communicated by headlines and radio-diffusion. People have to struggle with them in order to make the concepts their own. The mass-parroting of easy suggestions makes people feel lost in space though they may stammer the ideological formula. Those suggestions serve as an intellectual varnish right over the animal skin beneath. What we absorb passively never becomes an active principle in us.

The new peace of mind that will precede the peace in the world must be ushered into existence by a gigantic inner psychological conflict waged in the minds of every thinking and feeling individual. To prove fruitful, everyone must have the courage to challenge and balance the hostile and aggressive forces within himself.

This victory through inner balance will proclaim the maturity of mankind. Best of all, people will understand that the very word *peace* has a seductive, ambivalent meaning. It may mean the peace of sleep and passivity and subservience—or the peace of a strong inner balance, equanimity and inner freedom. The new heroic, difficult peace will be infinitely more majestic than any war

Notes

Footnotes to Chapter One

[1] News from Behind the Iron Curtain, Vol. 1, 1952.

Footnotes to Chapter Two

[1] Bergler, E. *The Basic Neurosis* New York Grune and Stratton, Inc. 1949.

Footnotes to Chapter Three

[1] *Sessions d'études de l'institut International des civilizations differentes.* Lisbonne. April, 1957.

[2] Hamdi Bey, "How Caste Survives," *Thought,* India, August 3, 1957.

Footnotes to Chapter Five

[1] It is difficult for a layman to find the "right" scientist to quote. Complicating this is government secrecy, which has the tendency of minimizing some dangers and presenting others through the prism of policy. The material here is derived from the following sources unless otherwise indicated.

H J Muller, "Genetic Damage Produced by Radiation," *Science,* Vol. 121, June, 1955.

Ch. Noel-Martin, Hat die Stunde H. geschlagen?

Ralph E. Lapp in *Bulletin of the Atomic Scientists,* June, 1955

W. F. Libby, "Radioactive Fallout and Medicine." *New York State Journal of Medicine,* April 15, 1959.

J. L. Kulp, A. R. Schulert and E. Y. Hodges, "Strontium 90 in Man." *Science*, Vol. 129, 1959

W. Schneir, "Strontium 90 in U S. Children." *The Nation*, April 25, 1959.

Puck, T. T., "Radiation and the Human Cell" *Scientific-American*, Vol. 202, April, 1960.

Fowler, J. M, *Fallout*. Basic Books New York, 1960.

[2] J. Besse and H. D. Lasswell, "Our Columnists and the A-Bomb," *World Politics*, Vol. III, 1950.

The Author

Dr. Joost A. M. Meerloo—psychoanalyst, author, teacher and former government official—is deeply aware of the urgency with which we must build peace. During the occupation of The Netherlands, where he was born and educated, he saw hate and fear at work, narrowly escaping death at the hands of the Nazis.

Born in 1903 at The Hague, Joost Meerloo earned his M.D. in 1927 at Leyden University and his Ph.D. in 1932 at the University of Utrecht. From 1928 to 1934, he served as teacher and staff psychiatrist in several hospitals, afterwards entering private practice in psychotherapy and acting as psychiatric consultant to the Royal Court and to governmental agencies in The Hague.

In 1942 he succeeded in escaping to England, where he served as chief of the Psychological Department of the Netherlands Army. Subsequently he was appointed High Commissioner for Welfare for the Netherlands Government, and was made an adviser to SHAEF and UNRRA. Dr. Meerloo was decorated with the Distinguished Service Cross in 1943.

After the war, Dr. Meerloo became a citizen of the United States. He has made his home in New York, where his private practice and teaching occupy much of his time. Dr. Meerloo's writings include more than 200 articles in both learned and popular journals, and 15 books—among them Total War and the Human Mind, The Two Faces of Man, Patterns of Panic, The Dance *and* The Rape of the Mind.

CPSIA information can be obtained
at www.ICGtesting.com
Printed in the USA
BVHW042140100521
607022BV00010B/199

9 780343 289386